The
EVERYTHING®
Guide to Raising Adolescent Girls

Dear Reader,

All the worries and struggles you experienced when your daughter was an infant and toddler will suddenly seem a snap when you begin to navigate your way through the adolescent years. This book is intended to help you on that journey. From when to expect physical changes and how to help your daughter (and you!) adapt to them, to how to deal with hot-button issues such as self-worth, dating, drinking, and more, this book will serve as your starting point, your guide and hopefully, your reassuring voice through a time that isn't always easy.

There's good news about you and this book: the fact that you're reaching out to educate and support yourself through your daughter's adolescent journey is proof that you are on the right track. As much as they try to push parents and guardians away during these years, the plain fact is your daughter needs your guidance and oversight in these years more than in any other.

And it's no afterthought that we've included a chapter on how to care for yourself in these years. No job is tougher—yet more rewarding—than raising a girl from innocent childhood to successful, confident and just plain wonderful adulthood. So here's to you: sit down, read on, and know you're on your way to helping your girl become a wonderful young woman.

Moira McCarthy

The EVERYTHING® Series

These handy, accessible books give you all you need to tackle a difficult project, gain a new hobby, or even brush up on something you learned back in school but have since forgotten. You can read cover to cover or just pick out information from the four useful boxes.

 Alerts: Urgent warnings

 Essentials: Quick handy tips

 Facts: Important snippets of information

 Questions: Answers to common questions

When you're done reading, you can finally say you know EVERYTHING®!

DIRECTOR OF INNOVATION Paula Munier

EDITORIAL DIRECTOR Laura M. Daly

EXECUTIVE EDITOR, SERIES BOOKS Brielle K. Matson

ASSOCIATE COPY CHIEF Sheila Zwiebel

ACQUISITIONS EDITOR Kerry Smith

DEVELOPMENT EDITOR Brett Palana-Shanahan

PRODUCTION EDITOR Casey Ebert

Visit the entire Everything® series at *www.everything.com*

THE

EVERYTHING®

GUIDE TO

RAISING ADOLESCENT GIRLS

Reassuring advice to help you and your
daughter navigate these turbulent years

Moira McCarthy with Mary E. Muscari, Ph.D., R.N.

avon, massachusetts

*For Leigh and Lauren—my two girls who took this
journey with me. Every moment has been worth it.*

• • •

An Everything® Series Book.
Everything® and everything.com® are registered
trademarks of F+W Publications, Inc.

Published by Adams Media, an F+W Publications Company
57 Littlefield Street, Avon, MA 02322 U.S.A.
www.adamsmedia.com

ISBN 10: 1-59869-442-1
ISBN 13: 978-1-59869-442-0

Printed in the United States of America.

J I H G F E D C B

Library of Congress Cataloging-in-Publication Data
is available from the publisher.

This publication is designed to provide accurate and authoritative information with
regard to the subject matter covered. It is sold with the understanding that the publisher is not engaged in rendering legal, accounting, or other professional advice.
If legal advice or other expert assistance is required, the services of a competent
professional person should be sought.
    —From a *Declaration of Principles* jointly adopted by a Committee of the
American Bar Association and a Committee of Publishers and Associations

Many of the designations used by manufacturers and sellers to distinguish their
products are claimed as trademarks. Where those designations appear in this book
and Adams Media was aware of a trademark claim, the designations have been
printed with initial capital letters.

*This book is available at quantity discounts for bulk purchases.
For information, please call 1-800-289-0963.*

Acknowledgments

Thank you Sean Stanford, a husband who was willing to learn how to French braid hair, drive to ballet, and understand all those "girl things" all these years. Thanks, also, to those families we have traveled this road with—the Jansson, Schranze, Lootz, Lincoln, Jordan and Mongello families; to all those girls at the Eel River Beach Club; to the Solers and the Tepps; to my Aunt Barbara Ohrenberger who set an example of how to be a great mother to girls (but who warned me while holding my first perfect baby girl: "She's so perfect. It's hard to believe she'll turn thirteen and tell you to go to heck!"). To the creators of Tab Energy, which continues to fuel me through long days of book writing. And to friends who are on the brink of all this: the Thompson's, The Clark Family, Paul and Jen Stanford, and the Tripp's, who are almost to the finish line. Thanks to my two girls: Leigh, a success in every way with sports, National Honor Society, and just plain being a wonderful young adult; and Lauren, who is still working her way through the teen years but has shown bravery in battling Type 1 Diabetes, and who was named the top middle school student in America with the Prudential Spirit of Community Award. I know you both will do so much good for the world. A special thanks too, to Ginny Irving and family, who have shown me grace, bravery, and what it really means to be remarkable people. Lillian Rose will be remembered forever.

Contents

Introduction

You've made it through the infant years, grabbing all the books you can get and finding support in baby groups. You've pretty much sailed through the early school years, when your daughter was compliant and wanting to please you at all times. For a moment—a brief moment—you thought "I did a good job; she turned out right." Maybe, once or twice, you witnessed the teen daughter of someone you know talking in a mean tone or disagreeing with her parent. You may have thought, "I'm glad my daughter isn't like that." Then comes adolescence, and much of it seems to have been thrown out the window. Fret not. The years of working to help her mold herself into a good adult were not for naught. But you still have more work to do. The adolescent years are challenging in every way. Your daughter may test you in ways you never imagined. She may lie when you never thought she would; she may try things you've clearly taught her are wrong. How is a parent to survive, and more importantly, how are parents to keep up their hard work and keep their daughter on the path to a healthy, happy adulthood, and a safe but meaningful adolescence? This book is designed to help you do just that. It should help you think through situations before they happen, keeping you on the ready. It should also help you to react to situations if you didn't see them coming. Teens are like "jumbo-sized" toddlers. While they push for freedom, they need you more than ever to be watching over them and yes, setting limits for them. This book should help you do just that. And someday, as rough as it seems now, you'll be able to hand it on to a friend and say, "I've been there and we made it through! Here's a guide to help you do the same."

Chapter 1

Where Has My Little Girl Gone?

It's hard not to fall into stereotypical expectations from the moment your baby girl is placed in your arms. You may want to cookie-cut your girl into the role you've been "media'd" into expecting, but in reality, girls can be anything from quiet to outspoken to athletic to submissive to arrogant to shy. Your first years of living with and raising your girl are of paramount importance to how the later years will go. Looking back, some parents wonder: did I try to force her into a role? Others look for clues as to what habits and actions early in life led her to being the adolescent she is today.

Sugar and Spice?

It starts in your hospital recovery room. Friends and family shower you with frocks, tiny tea sets, and first dolls. Even parents who didn't know the sex of their child and play it safe with the yellow or beige nursery decor find themselves filling it with pink once that baby girl calls it home. There is no question that parents, despite their desire to be neutral in who their children become, make tiny, subliminal moves from the first day that help send messages to their daughter's mind: you *are* a female.

Historical Images of What Being a "Girl" Means

Not long ago, girls were treated in a way that was drastically different from the way boys were treated. In the grand scheme of time, fainting couches, corsets, and no formal education are fairly recent history. And somewhere in the collective unconscious, the echoes of that philosophy may still exist.

Think about it: many parents of teen girls reading this book are probably old enough to remember when girl's gym class and boy's gym class were two totally different programs. Boys would romp hard and aggressive out on the field. Girls would learn calisthenics in the quiet gym. Even dress codes set girls apart. Sure, boys couldn't wear shorts or ratty clothing, but girls could not wear pants.

This was only part of the issue. Not too long ago, girls were not expected to excel at math, and some parents still held onto the belief that with a good secretarial job after high school a girl would be fine until marriage. At birthday parties, girls were expected to get art sets and dolls, yet boys were all about bows and arrows and sporting goods. And while you may like to think you're nothing like that anymore, being raised in and around this mentality has left an indelible mark on your psyche. Somewhere deep down, you may still think "sugar and spice and everything nice" when you think girls.

The "Modern" Image

And so today, when that little baby is placed in your arms, you like to think you are open to anything for her. Soccer balls are placed next to her crib. You read long and hard about how girls can excel in any subject matter and you introduce them to words and numbers and kicking a ball in the yard from the earliest days. But are you truly all that modern? As Judith Jack Halberstam points out so clearly, people still do tend to categorize girls as softer and sweeter than boys. Who hasn't taped a bow on their little bald baby girl's head and sung those "sugar and spice and everything nice" words to her?

 Fact

According to gender scholar Judith Jack Halberstam, some stereotypical gender differentiation may still exist: for example, younger girls can roughhouse with little repercussion, but the term "tomboy" is still often attached to adolescent girls who are not "girly girls."

Could this be because society still, somewhere deep down, craves that nursery rhyme's simplistic take on females? And one has to wonder: why is it that tiny little boys seem to tend naturally toward toy trucks and cars and girls toward dolls and paints? It's a question all parents of girls have to ask themselves as they work at guiding their tiny little girl through the pitfalls of growing up.

The Years Before Adolescence

The early years with your daughter can be a joyful challenge, just as they are with any child. You'll get your share of what you dreamed of: tea parties with her tiny playmates, cheering for her at Tumble Tots, and watching with joy as she begins to remember book themes, numbers, and other "amazing feats." The challenge for today's mom and dad is finding a way, in those early years, to mix your own dreams with a realistic role for your daughter in today's world. If you're reading this, you've most likely already been through those years, so a look at what you did, how you role modeled, and what you can learn from it can be useful at this time.

Toddler Girls

The toddlers years are full of playgroups, dress up, and challenging days of learning and growing. For little girls, parents often focus on "role playing games" such as "house" and "tea party." Playtime usually means hanging out with little girls from the neighborhood or that you've met through day care, but boys aren't so drastically different that they cannot be entered into the mix as well. But how often, in those early play days with the cute little boy down the street, did you and the other parent joke about showing the photos of that day at their wedding? People seemed programmed to think forward to a future male-female relationship. Did your daughter pick up on that?

It's easy to think back on these days as stress-free, despite the issues of temper tantrums, potty training, and the like. After all, can you imagine if all it took to make your teen girl happy today was letting her run around in circles wearing her dress-up shoes for a few minutes? While toddler girls were a challenge, they were also a joy. The seemingly constant moments of discovery (She can write her name! She knows how to do a somersault!) helped buoy you through more stressful times. And back then, the future was a blank slate, something you were working to paint the best picture on. In almost every case, your daughter had yet to say she disliked you, and chances are, she still worshipped the ground you walked on. If you were giddy with the glee of success, do not feel alone. More than a few parents have looked at their coming-out-of-toddlerhood girls and thought, "I've done this right. I've raised a perfect girl."

 Essential

Take time to sit down with your daughter and look over old family photos from her early years. Weave into the conversation games she played, ways she thought, and how she had friendships with boys at that time. This will convey to her that she's a unique individual and not just "sugar and spice."

Early School Years

As their daughter grows, parents begin to sense a change. Some lament the "influence of the outside world" on their daughter's attitudes; others struggle to keep control of their lives through volunteering at school and helping out with after school and sports activities. But no matter how you try, your daughter is going to begin to develop her own opinions, her own beliefs, and yes, disagreements with you. Fifth grade seems to be a common age for girls to begin showing some push-back at parents. It also seems to be the time when girl-versus-girl conflicts, like cliques and battles and jostling over "liking boys," begin to surface.

Sixth or seventh grade usually signals the beginning of middle school—prime time for changes, struggles, and issues in a girl's life. Parents who may be looking forward to less stress in raising a girl should actually be ready for the opposite. The more available a parent can be in these years, the better for the child.

Wishes Versus Reality

Everyone has dreams: it's one of the reasons people bring children into the world in the first place. Some parents imagine their daughter playing in the U.S. Open, and her first tennis racquet is propped up next to her crib before she's born. Other parents dream of their daughter being a valedictorian, and so those Baby Einstein tapes are placed in order from the first day. It's not wrong to have dreams for how your daughter will be. But knowing how to balance your dreams with the person she chooses to become is the trick.

Wishes for Her or Wishes for You?

All parents have to ask themselves: are my wishes for my daughter more for me or for her? It's hard *not* to live your life vicariously through your daughter. After all, your adolescence was riddled with disappointments (if it wasn't, you are truly unique in that feat). Perhaps you were never student council president, you didn't make varsity soccer, or, you did make varsity soccer and loved every minute of it. Maybe you hated when your parents forced you to take piano, or you always wanted to take piano and your parents could not afford it. No matter what the issue, chances are that much of what you wish for your daughter you are subconsciously wishing for your own long-gone teenaged self.

And there's nothing wrong with wanting to introduce your daughter to the things you loved and try to steer her away from things that caused you pain. But from an early age, you need to remember that your child is not your mini-me.

 *Question*

Is all lost if my daughter hates what I love at an early age?
If your daughter balked at an activity or skill you dreamed of her loving as a small child, reintroduce it when she's a teen. Tastes change. She may just find she likes it after all. Don't assume an early childhood decision sticks with a girl for life.

And so, as she grows, it is important for you to take stock in what you are asking her to do. Does she really want to be the goalie of the most aggressive middle school soccer team in the area, or is she just trying to please you by making your wish come true? Hard as it may be, try to not to get too excited about the things you secretly wish for. Nothing is more painful than a girl pushing herself somewhere she does not want to be because she wants to win Mom or Dad's love by making their wishes come true.

Relationship Wishes

You grew up watching those TV parents always being able to have calm, meaningful, and successful talks with their girls. In your dreams, your daughter grows up talking to you about everything, taking in your sage advice, and always knowing she can be honest with you. You'll be not just her parent, but also her best friend. You know it from the start.

 Alert

> What you are learning now, as your daughter grows, is that growing smarter and more independent often means lashing out at the person you trust and love the most, and that would be you. Because they trust you, they can be at their worst with you.

This is the hardest wish of all to let go of. But instead of letting go, you'll need to rethink what it means to have a wonderful parent-daughter relationship (see Chapter 2 for details).

So should you let go of those now seemingly crazy wishes you had when they were young? Not at all. Having dreams not only for your child but also for your relationship with your child is natural and healthy. You just may need to rethink the execution of those wishes, and the time frame in which they will come true. Even in the rough years, and even when she might not be acting as kindly to you as you wish, you are always your child's strongest supporter and most loved person. As you navigate the waters of adolescence, keeping that in mind may just be the rudder you need to keep you steered toward your final goal: a well-raised adult who respects and loves her parents, family, and friends. Just know, the seas will get choppy.

Your Little Girl Is Growing Up

In reality it happens slowly, but for many parents, the idea of their little girl growing up hits fast and hard. There are signs: her body begins to stretch out and be leaner; her attitude seems to shift suddenly from time to time. These times of change will cause internal and external stress to your daughter, and will challenge you to adapt your parenting skills.

Physical Changes

You've heard it said: puberty seems to be coming earlier and earlier for today's girls. Some studies point to the average age of the onset of puberty being a full year earlier than it was a half century ago, naming increased body mass index (BMI), as a possible reason. Whatever age your child starts, the beginning signs are usually the same.

Girls usually have a sudden surge in height (but not necessarily weight) at the very start of puberty. A year or more after that, girls begin to notice a darkening of the areola and the growth of a small mound at the breasts (called "buds"). This can be a surprise to the child, and the parent, and a particularly challenging time for the father (see Chapter 3 for more on fathers and dealing with development).

It is not unusual for one breast to grow faster than another, causing worry to the child. In addition, hands and feet grow faster than the rest of the body, which can mean a so-called "clumsy" time for a girl. Tennis star Maria Sharapova was young enough when she became a world champ to have gone through this before the eyes of the tennis-loving world. For a time, she had trouble moving to the ball. In time, her body caught up to itself and she returned to being the best in the world.

Pubic hair comes next, something some girls announce and others are embarrassed by. In any case, this development is proof that you are well into your life of having a child in puberty. While some girls may think this is a sign that her first period will be days away, in fact, only 20 percent of girls experience a first period at the first signs of pubic hair.

 Essential

It's an old classic, and it got you through this time, and the good news is, while dated, it still works. Buy your daughter Judy Bloom's *Are You There God? It's Me, Margaret* before she goes through this time of adolescence.

This is the time, too, when girls begin to experience things like body odor and acne. It is important to stay ahead of the curve with your daughter on these issues. Help her understand and practice good hygiene habits before she finds herself in an embarrassing situation. A "Shaving 101" lesson with mom (or another female in her life) is a good idea as well, since many girls will try—and botch—this necessary practice on their own.

You and your daughter may notice, too, an increase in body fat. Early pubescent girls can almost look "puffy" at times. It is important to share with your daughter, if she brings it up, that this is a perfectly normal part of development and that, as her height catches up, she'll find her body balances things for her (with healthy eating and an active lifestyle).

The Big "P"

Take a deep breath and shake out those nerves because, it's going to happen: eventually, your daughter will get her period. Being prepared for this major moment in life and knowing how to treat it with dignity and intelligence is one of the most vital things a parent can do for a daughter.

 Alert

A girl's weight or activity level can affect when a period starts or does not start. If you are concerned that your daughter's period should have started, consult her health care provider.

By the time any girl is two years prior to the possibility of puberty, she should be well versed in what a period is, how it will begin, and what she should do about it. True, schools today to a good job of educating girls (and boys) on such issues, but she needs to hear it from you. Not only will this ensure that the two of you are on the same page, but perhaps more importantly, it will open the lines of communication between you on the topic.

When you do address the issue, be sure to let her know that a period in no way needs to interrupt her life or keep her from doing any of the activities she enjoyed before starting her period.

Girls will want to know, before they even need them, how and why to use all types of sanitary products. Particularly with tampons, where misuse runs the real risk of the dangerous toxic shock syndrome, girls need to be shown firsthand how to use supplies and how often to change them. Don't take anything for granted. And if it's uncomfortable or embarrassing for you or your child, just deal with it. The act of being open and honest, yet respectful, can lay the groundwork for sharing information on this and other topics in the future.

If your daughter refuses to discuss this at all, leave literature around the house about it. Give her the chance to read the information you provide. At least you'll know she's read some information.

 Fact

Believe it or not, even in this era of information, your daughter may still be shocked by her body's changes. Always be sure to remind her that it is normal; all girls go through these changes.

And what about "celebrating" a period? Some modern moms believe in it, but take your child's wishes to heart. Some girls just don't want you posting a banner reading, "Little Anna is a woman now!" A quiet gift or a special outing for, say, a pedicure might be enough. Or, your child may prefer to just go on with life. Periods are, after all, just another part of life.

Describe cramping and premenstrual syndrome (PMS) to your daughter as well, and encourage her to share with you if she has any of these feelings. Let her know that there are ways to easily relieve it, and if such symptoms become severe, you'll be on the ready to find a good solution for her.

Emotional Changes

There's an old saying: an adolescent girl is really just a toddler in a bigger body, and that's not too far from true. The emotional changes that growing girls go through, caused by hormonal fluctuation, peer pressure, and just plain figuring out who she is in relation to you, her friends, and the world can be the roller-coaster ride of a lifetime. The challenge for parents is knowing why it's happening, what to expect, and most of all, how to react.

Some parents can remember the moment they first saw the emotional change in their daughter. An outburst or mini-breakdown about something that seems inconsequential to parents rocks the girl's world. Others find it creeps up on them: their sunny, always cooperative daughter is suddenly sullen and argumentative many times. Either way, the emotional changes during adolescence can be as frightening and confusing to the parent as they can be to the daughter.

Girls who were even-keeled and able to take on so much suddenly may be quick to snap in a harsh way at parents or in an emotional way with friends or at school. Don't be surprised if most of it is focused at you, the parent. There's a simple reason: children tend to test out new behaviors where they know they are safe. You love your child, and your child knows it. So when she snaps at you or speaks disparagingly, try (and this is a challenge) to see it as a sign of trust and love.

 Question

How do I know if emotional changes are "normal"?
Many parents mistake the emotions of puberty with something more serious. If you have concerns, your best bet is a talk with your daughter's health care provider.

Girls may find at this time too that holding it together all day long in school is a burden. Many parents find, almost immediately after school, they witness "meltdowns." This can be the pent up emotions she's been holding back all day long. It's a challenge for parents to find ways to channel that and help their daughter work through it. (More on this in Chapter 7).

Thought Processes as She Grows

When your daughter was little, she was a clean slate, ready and open for you to suggest how she thinks and what she thinks. Now, she's exposed to a whole world beyond you. Friends, enemies, teachers, television, music, and films all play a role in suggesting to her what and how she thinks about the world. In a time when everything is in question and her hormones make everything seem magnified, you may wonder if anything you've instilled in her is still there. It is. It just needs care and feeding.

"But My Friends Say . . ."

Remember when you could point to a tree, say "That's a maple," and she'd say, "And a beautiful maple it is!" With adolescence comes doubt; doubt born in what she hears from friends, who seemingly rule her world. Today you could point at that same tree, and you'd hear, "Jenny says that those really aren't trees at all. They're sticks. Don't you know *anything?*" This is because your daughter's thought process is moving toward a place where she simply does not take your word—or anyone else's if that makes you feel any better—as law.

Girls have to move from a place of total trust in one being (usually the parent) to a trust in herself. As you notice your daughter leaning more and more toward using what her friends say as a vital part in her thought process, you'll be tempted to snap something like "Jenny's a dolt!," or, "I don't want you hanging out with her anymore!" Rather, the best bet is to show that you're willing to listen to what the friend's point of view is, then point out to your daughter why you feel yours is important. This will help your child learn to balance what she takes in and come to her own hopefully smart-thinking conclusions.

Reactionary Thinking

Girls at this age can snap to quick—and not always the best—thoughts. Remember, girls this age live in the moment.

Like the toddler who cannot understand that the family trip to Disney next month is actually thirty days away and not in a minute, adolescent girls think every thing they think over or consider is the absolute end of the world.

 Alert

Arguing is not the answer. You'll need to find a positive way to show your daughter how to use her thought process to come to the right conclusions. Even concerning something as simple as "what kind of tree is that," be calm and find a way to agree without a battle (which can be easier said than done).

So how do you teach a girl to avoid thinking this way? That may be impossible. But, by making sure she is safe and unable to put herself in situations that can come from rash decisions, you'll at least be secure in knowing she'll make it through this phase. And sometimes, that's the best you can do.

Chapter 2

Life with Mom

For you—and possibly for your daughter—the notion of the mother-daughter relationship has been fantasized about. In your mind (thanks to the media and the tall tales of friends) you share everything. When she's confused, she always turns to you. When you suspect something may be amiss in her life, you sit her down for a calm, rational, and productive heart-to-heart. The reality is the mother-daughter relationship is one of the most trying to navigate. But, your work at building this relationship in a positive way is key to your daughter's successful voyage through adolescence.

Your Relationship with Your Daughter

It's not always easy to remember when dealing with an adolescent girl that you are the *adult* in the relationship. So many mothers want to use their relationship with their daughter to "make up" for something they missed with their own mother or repeat something they loved there that they lose sight of one simple fact: your daughter, and therefore your relationship with her, is unique.

Media Manipulation

Carol and the Brady girls. That mom on *Gilmore Girls*. Just about every mother who graced a big screen, leaving aside *Mommy Dearest* (who did nothing for our image of how mothers appear when they are not quite sane with their girls). Today's moms have been bombarded with images of how to expect their relationship with their daughters to unfold. Sure, there will be hard times (even Laura Ingalls disagreed with Caroline from time to time), but overall, moms hope to be with their daughter be like two peas in a pod; two beings who share, learn and grow together. What happens on TV or film isn't real, yet it sinks into the public subconscious and plays with personal expectations.

 Essential

Try to train yourself to let those expectations go. After all, you watched *Star Wars* and didn't expect a visit from Han Solo. It's no more realistic to expect a perfect relationship with your daughter.

If you look closer at the media—and at the actual actors who play the parts—you'll see more reality. Brooke Shields had a trying-at-best relationship with her mother for a time. Jennifer Aniston is still trying to figure hers out. And Dinah and Lindsay Lohan? That type of situation is addressed in the later section on "trying to be a cool mom." Instead of looking toward Tinseltown for role models for your relationship, build your own. Expect bumps; be ready for a roller coaster ride. But know it's all for the best.

Who You Are to Her

When she was little, you were like a Goddess. Anything you did—pulling weeds, taking her to playgroups, reading her a book—seemed like the best thing anyone could ever do. Now, she's growing and developing her own ideas, and they aren't always the right ideas. You—if you are doing your job as a mom—have begun to become more of a rule maker. While she once looked to you for every answer, she may begin to come at you with her own answers—answers you have to strongly correct. From what to wear to where to go to how to act, she sees you as a controller. And in many ways, you are. The important thing for mothers to realize at this hard time of transition in their mother-daughter relationship is this: somewhere deep down, despite her anger or pushing back, she knows you are the person who loves and protects her.

 Fact

It's a good idea to have some kind of "positive moment" with your daughter at least once a week. Whether it's out for tea together or a walk, insist on it, no matter how much she pushes back. This will help you (and her) hold onto some of that feeling you crave.

It can be hard—almost heartbreaking—for a mother to transition to the role of enforcer, but in order for a girl to grow up smart, strong, successful, and safe, it's a must. Anyone who watches *The Sopranos* remembers the year Meadow got caught sneaking out her window and was denied her trip to Aspen the next week. Meadow seemed to *hate* her mother for the punishment, but the mother held strong (and kept her tears to herself). She was showing her daughter that when it came to rules for her safety, she meant business, no matter how tough it was. All mothers need to do the same. Your relationship to your daughter should be loving, caring, and most of all, guiding in the right direction, no matter how rough the seas can get.

Your Image of Her Life

All mothers visualize the girl (and even woman) their daughter will be, from the day of conception and sometimes even before that. You see her as a star athlete, long braids bouncing along as she attacks a ski trail or completes a lay up on the basketball court. Or she's the star of all the school plays. You know she'll be an artist, like her grandmother was. Whatever your dream of who she will be, it is important to remember that while your dreams are not forbidden, neither are they a sure thing.

Piece of Clay

Marvin Gaye sang it just right in one of his early tunes, "Everybody's got somebody, to be their own piece of clay." All daughters start out, parents believe, as putty in their hands. Parents expose them to what they want to—be it music, books, sports or all of the above—and hope they latch onto the characteristics and interests that parents dream them to. It is important for a mother to work hard at (and this is not always simple) separating her image of her daughter's life from what her daughter eventually decides she wants her life to be.

Let's say you were class president. Being active and outspoken was a part of your adolescence, one you hope your daughter emulates. So, from a young age, you expose her to volunteerism, civic duty, and speaking out for herself and for others. But what if your daughter is, pure and simply, shy? It is important in these growing years that you listen to what your child wants and make sure she never feels obligated to act like someone or something she is not comfortable being. It's her skin, not yours.

 Alert

Pushy youth-sport parents can do more harm for adolescent girls than good. Sports should be about fun, not about future scholarships or your unfulfilled dreams. Always leave it up to your daughter if she participates or not.

Don't be surprised if you find your daughter wanting to *not* be exactly like you. Being totally connected to her mother as part of her image was a part of her youth; pushing away from it is a step toward independence. Some liberal Democrat mothers find their daughters leaning at a young age toward Republicanism. Other mothers notice their daughters wanting to dress differently from them for a time. But don't think she's not paying attention, and even secretly respecting, what you say, do, and feel. In the end, the values you've instilled should shine through.

Physical Image

Does your daughter look just like you? Sound just like you? Even in the case of adopted children, family traits can show through. As your daughter develops, look for her to want to push away from your image and be her own person.

Some girls do this with clothing (although most moms find that fashion is cyclical; if you wore it twenty-five years ago, chances are your teen is calling it new and hip today). Encourage your daughter to express herself with style, within reason.

If you have weight issues, be sure to be open with your daughter about them. Let her see photos of you at her age, whether you were thin or overweight, and talk to her about a healthy way to look the way she wants. You don't want your daughter fearing weight gain if you gained it after having children, or struggling to be thinner when her bone structure is smaller than yours. Enlist your health care provider to help her understand what is healthy for *her* body rather than for yours or anyone else's. Even if you imagine her to be a perfect size four, show her how she can dress well at any size. And make sure she knows she's loved for who she is, not what she looks like.

Her Image of What Her Life Should Be

Your teen girl probably has as many externally suggested images of what she should be like as you do. Teens today are assaulted by more advertising images than ever before. For an insecure teen girl (and is there any other kind of teen girl?) it can all be a bit overwhelming.

Physical Expectations

For as long as Barbie dolls have marched off the production line—and perhaps even longer than that—girls have been assaulted with mixed messages of what their bodies should look like. They should be rail thin, yet have round and perky breasts. Their skin should be clear. Their hair should be highlighted with some sort of glimmering color, and they should always be put together.

Trying to even be one tiny part of this impossible picture can be both physically and emotionally damaging to adolescent girls.

 *Question*

What do I do if I find my daughter is stuffing her bra?
Don't freak out. Instead, use real life examples of how many wonderful and successful people have many kinds of body shapes. Encourage her to let her own unique shape shine.

In the early years, these issues often come in the form of girls wanting to be more grown-up. Bra stuffing is alive and well, and with today's "miracle bras" and padded bras that will make a girl look larger earlier, it's even easier to pull off. While such actions certainly have no physical implications, think of the emotional consequences: allowing your daughter to feel, at a young age, that she needs to alter her appearance for acceptance is a dangerous message. Any young woman— and any person at all for that matter—needs to grow up loving themselves for who they are. Acceptance of things like bra stuffing as "just normal" works directly against that goal.

And then there is today's bra stuffing: breast implants. It's true. Teen girls are considering—and in some cases parents are allowing—breast augmentation at an early age. Parents need to know that, according to the American Society of Plastic Surgeons, the Food and Drug Administration has not approved breast augmentation for youth under age eighteen. There are more reasons to say no to this than psychological (what are you saying to your child if you tell her she needs to go under a knife for acceptance?). There are physical dangers as well.

Make-up 101

Remember when you were her age and all you knew of makeup was Loves Baby Soft and Bonne Bell clear lip gloss? Makeup companies market directly at younger teen girls today, and it's hard for our girls to resist. A good idea is to find a quality spa in your area and do a "junior facial." Ask the aesthetician ahead of time to help your daughter learn to care for her skin and look lovely *without* makeup for these early years. Make the investment in good skin care products and encourage her to let her wonderful, changing self shine through.

It also may be a good idea to accept that there is a good chance your daughter is going to want to wear some makeup. Rather than having her sneak it (the girls bathroom of the middle school can be a haven of makeup application moments), show her the correct way to use makeup and how and when to remove it each day. Make sure you purchase her quality products that will help and not hurt her delicate skin.

Social Expectations

Girls grow up with dreams of their lives just as you have dreams for them. For many girls, the reality can seem harshly different than their dreams. They find, quickly, that they are not indeed Paris Hilton or Beyoncé, or maybe not even the sports star or queen of the school they so wanted to be. Helping your daughter understand who she is and what her wonderful strengths are is a key job for Mom in these years.

There is the rare girl who grows up happy to be in the skin she is in: cliques, sports teams, certain parties; none of it matters to her. But most girls do struggle in these years with how they want their social worlds to be. Some of this might come from you, even if you don't realize it.

For the mom who was unpopular as a teen girl, this can be a chance at what seems to be redemption. The cool girls shut her out, but now her daughter will be *the* cool girl, she thinks. Your child is smart enough to catch onto this, and that can be harmful. Even in their most difficult years, girls love their mothers and want to please them. If your daughter senses you want her to be the star and she does not make it there, she'll feel a double whammy: her disappointment and yours.

It's a good idea at this age too, to let your daughter know a simple truth: no one wants to peak in middle school or even high school. Be honest with her about things that were rough for you too; show her how you and others she knows got through these years and came into who they are over a long period of time. No one, in other words, is trapped in her middle school or high school image. The girl who can truly understand this (and there are few) is the one who can deal with this difficult time of life with grace. Your assurance that even though she was not invited to Perfect Paula's end of year bash, she'll still grow to be a beloved and successful person might be met with tears and a "You don't know!" but inside, those words will resonate. Be sure to assure her constantly.

 Essential

If you had a particularly difficult adolescence and you can still feel the acute pain of it today, it's a good idea to check in with some counseling for yourself. Truly doing what is best for your child means putting aside—and working out—what was broken in you in the past.

No Such Thing as the "Cool Mom"

The so-called "Cool Mom," often self-anointed as such, isn't a character you need turn to Hollywood to see. Chances are there's a Cool Mom wannabe right in your own neighborhood or school district. And chances are she's making other moms' lives just about miserable.

What Drives the "Cool Mom"

The Cool Mom thinks of herself as more of her daughter's friend than as her parent. Her goal is to be popular herself, and to do so, she'll resort to almost anything: making outrageous purchases, showing a complete disregard for any kind of discipline, and acting like she's the mom all the other girls in town can "come to talk" at any time. Moms have many different motivations for wanting to serve this role, and at the end of the day, none of them have to do with what is best for their children. Cool moms are often looking to fill other voids in their lives. Maybe they were lonely as children. Maybe they want more than anything for their daughter to treat them like an equal. Whatever the case, these moms, with their late curfews, coed sleepovers, and readily accessible birth control for their daughters are more than misguided.

Girls can be wowed by these moms. Think about it: all the rules you are enforcing and the "tough love" you are practicing for true and correct reasons can seem completely wrong to her if her friend's mom just lets her do what she wants. Happiness is in the moment in these years, and your daughter does not understand that your way is in fact the best way. It may take time, but at some point, your daughter will hopefully see that often, the rules and "uncool" things you do are actually in her best interest, and are what truly show love to a child.

Why You Cannot Be the Cool Mom

It might be tempting to go down this road, but you must not. Why can't you just be the cool mom? Put simply, because your daughter's health, safety, and future depend on you resisting it.

The role of mom in her daughter's adolescent years is far from fun. As discussed earlier, in most cases, you've long past that time of getting constant admiration and adoration from her. This can hurt the mother's psyche. After all, parents want their children to worship them. But here's where being a grown-up comes in: you must stick to the rules and limitations your daughter needs placed on her in these important years. Even if she sometimes (okay, more than sometimes) seems to resent you for it, the payoff will come down the road when she's a well-adjusted and successful young adult who at that point, by the way, will absolutely think you really were the coolest mother ever.

 Alert

Don't let a cool mom "steal" your daughter away. If you find yourself in a situation, confront the mother in person and alone and let her know that your rules for your child extend to her house too.

Your Changing Relationship

It may seem to change in an afternoon, or it may shift slowly over time. But your relationship with your daughter will most likely shift in these challenging years. Knowing how to shift with it and keep it on track as a loving one is one of your most important roles as a mother.

"I Love You!"

For years now, she's been willing to kiss you goodbye in front of anyone, yell "I love you!" at any time, and might even suddenly hug you for no reason right smack in the middle of the grocery store/soccer dome/street. Now, she moves away from you to avoid a kiss goodbye when you drop her off somewhere, and turns beet red when you say those now-dreaded three words: I love you. So, you wonder, when and why did she stop loving you? She hasn't. Not even in the least. In fact, these are the years she loves you and needs you most, even though ironically, she seldom (if ever) shows it.

 Essential

When you first notice your daughter not wanting any public displays of affection or "PDAs" with you, devise a secret "I love you signal." A discreet double squeeze of the palm is enough, so long as you two know the meaning.

As much as you'd like her to still show the world she adores you, it is most natural for a girl to grow to not display these things for everyone all the time. It is important, though, for you to find a way to express your love, and for her to express hers, comfortably. It's easy to slide into assuming someone does not care about you if they never hear it from you. And if you just let it go, years from now, your daughter could say, "You never told me you loved me." Finding a way to keep that part of your evolving relationship alive that she is comfortable with will remind her you do always love her. (And for you hearing or feeling her love at times other than when a cash register and your credit card are involved). If you can find an easy and agreeable solution, this is one place where, while your relationship shifts, it does not have to truly change.

It is important, too, for you to continue finding ways to express love to your child because you are her role model. You want her to grow into an adult who feels free expressing her opinions and showing the world her love. If you freeze up now because she does, she'll model that behavior. If you adapt and find new ways, she'll model that instead. No, it's not normal for you to run after the high school bus blowing kisses or to give her a giant hug goodbye when you drop her off at the football game, but it is normal to give her a kiss goodnight, every night, at home. Don't shy away from the simple, private acts of love just because she wants to. In the end, she'll be glad you did not.

 Fact

This is one time when texting can be good. Kids might not want to say "I love you," but they are more than happy to text ILU (text slang for I love you) just about any time.

"I Hate You!"

As sure as the sun is going to shine, your teen daughter is going to tell you she hates you. Be ready for it. How is a parent to react? While you cannot ignore it, neither can you allow it to almost end the world. Hate is a strong word and one that you've most likely raised your child to clearly understand the implication of yet, somewhere around twelve or thirteen years old, there it comes: hurling past her lips and right at your face. It's shocking and it's hurtful, but that's your child's goal. Of course she does not hate you, but she's confused or upset and you, good parent, are her "safe spot," a place where she can let out as much angst as she wants and never, ever be cast away.

So what's a sensitive parent to do? The first step is to defuse the situation. Yelling back is not a solution. Tell your child you want to be alone—or for her to be alone—until she can talk to you rationally. When she can (even if it's hours later), remind her of how harmful a word like "hate" is, and that you do not allow it to be used that way in your home. Then, expect her to do it again sometime. Because she will.

You may notice too that your daughter tries to choose one parent as the "hated" and one as the favorite. Do not allow this to happen, as it is manipulation it one of its clearest forms, and not a good practice for your daughter to have success in. (More on how to parent as a true team in Chapter 6).

 *Question*

What if she really does hate me?
If the "hate" talk and feelings are more than just fleeting and from time to time, family counseling is in order. Anger—in any prolonged form—should always be addressed and adjusted.

And what about how you feel? With your daughter not wanting to hug you, being willing to say she hates you, and avoiding you in many cases, moms can begin to feel their own feelings of abandonment at most and under-appreciation at least. The key here is to remember that many, if not most, girls go through this. You probably did at one point in your life with your own mother, and it will pass. So long as you stay strong as a parent, stick to what she needs and love her all the while, things will shift to a new level of love. It just takes time. In the end, the coolest thing a mom can do is work hard to help her adolescent girl navigate her way through these choppy years and come out a whole, happy, well-adjusted adult.

Chapter 3

Life with Dad

In the early years, little girls talk of marrying their daddies and dads put their daughters on a pedestal. But in the adolescent years, the father-daughter relationship shifts through so many changes, it's hard to keep track. Girls learn early to manipulate their dads and dads begin, as girls grow to young women, to worry about how to act around the child they used to feel so free around. The challenge for the dad is finding a new and appropriate closeness with his daughter.

Daddy's Little Girl

It's the most requested father-daughter dance song at American weddings, so it's no surprise that most fathers and daughters fill these dual roles. Every dad wants his daughter to be "Daddy's little girl." And for the first years that's a snap. It's when they begin to grow into young women that things get dicey.

Physical Changes

It's easy when daughters are prepubescent for fathers to not obsess about the physical issues of any male-to-female relationship. Little girls are not that much different than little boys, and while dads do realize they'll someday develop, it's easy to put that out of mind.

So when the first flush of breast growth or other female signs of maturity begin to show, some fathers can feel challenged.

It is usually at this time a father will begin to pull back physically from a daughter. Ironically, in this time of transformation and personal confusion, a daughter may need to feel her relationship with her father stay steady more than ever. So what's a father to do? It's all about adaptation.

 Essential

As your daughter learns about her body changes from her mother and from school, make sure you are part of this education as well. Open discussion from day one will make things more comfortable for you two as you head down the road to her female maturity.

While you once bounced her on your lap every day after work, there comes a time when this is simply not acceptable anymore. But that does not mean you cannot show physical affection. A hug hello and a peck on the cheek each day after work is always a good choice—even if she begins to pull back. Show her you love her, and that you can express that properly to her even as she grows. If she starts to be standoffish about this, discuss a "secret code signal," as discussed in Chapter 2. A quiet hand squeeze or something else as unviewable to the public can serve to remind her you do love her and do want to tell her.

 Fact

Dads are not supposed to talk and communicate just like moms. Let your own way and relationship develop with your daughter, and leave the mom role to Mom.

The "Big P" and Dad

Some girls are willing to let their fathers know they've gotten their periods; others are embarrassed. It's the father's lead that will make the difference here. Make sure she knows you understand the changes she is going through, and that while you respect her privacy, you also care about her well-being, both physically and emotionally, in this changing time. Single fathers will want to make sure they have all the supplies their daughter will need on hand well before they are needed. Place sanitary supplies in an easy to access spot and then let her know the items she might need are there. Find a close female relative or friend—anyone your daughter respects and trusts—and ask her to serve that role for your daughter at this time. Let your daughter know this woman does not replace you as the parent in this situation, but is there to support her as you perhaps cannot.

Every dad, married or single, needs to keep an open line of dialogue with his daughter about her changes, such as periods. Even if it feels awkward, just let her know you understand. But don't ever do it in an embarrassing way, like talking about it in front of friends and even other relatives. Let her know you respect her privacy, but that you indeed are part of that private world. At the same time, give her space. While she once used to come out of the shower with you standing there, she will now need privacy. Make sure she has robes to wear and a lock on her bathroom door. Everyone deserves that safety net.

Emotional Changes

When girls are small, they are still emotional, but their emotions are less complex and easier for fathers to navigate. When they experience fear, Dad is there to make them feel safe. They get their feelings hurt in simple ways and Dad is there to boost them up again. Being left out of a play date can be solved with an ice cream trip or even a few pushes on the swings. But as she grows into the mysterious world of girls and their actions, Dad may begin to feel clueless.

Fathers may find, as their girls grow into the era of peer pressure and cliques that they want to lash out to protect their daughters. It's important to find a balance. Let her know you care but don't step into the fray of girl nonsense. Weigh the situation and then deal with it by helping your daughter figure out how to work things out on her own but with your insight. She'll see you care and that you understand, but most of all, that you trust her to work it out.

And what of the emotional changes that you just plain don't get? A girl's hormones can wreak havoc on her in these years, and that's something it is near impossible for a father to empathize with. Don't explain every action away by saying "it must be hormones." Rather, try to help your daughter learn to find ways to work out her feelings without lashing out or freaking out. Walks, throwing the ball, even suggesting some quiet time alone in her room until she calms down can all help her learn to cope with feelings in a positive way. Making suggestions on how to vent anger might be met with another screech, but in time, she will hopefully catch on. If you have to, drag her out to do something to relieve the stress. Your knowing what to suggest will show her that males can be sensitive and understanding—a good example to set for any girl.

 Alert

If your daughter ends up in a situation in which you fear she may be physically harmed, it is time to step in. But always do it with the other children's parents, and teachers, if possible, involved. Do not take on teen girl issues with just the teen girls.

The Importance of a Father in a Girl's Life

Not every girl has a father present in her life, and yet, a father figure of some kind can do so much to help a girl as she grows. If you are a single mother, you'll want to think these things over as your daughter grows. And if you are a father, it does you good to assess why you are needed and why you are there.

The Traditional Father

You're married to your child's mother, and you've been so for the child's entire life. You are the traditional father. Your role is easier than that of some other fathers, but that does not mean it's simple. Traditional fathers, like mothers, may have cookie-cutter images of how they expect life to be with their daughter. Working toward the relationship you two unique humans were meant to have will not only fulfill you, but it will help your daughter learn how to work toward a healthy relationship with all men, a necessary skill for any woman, be she single, married, gay, or straight. Your daughter will have to deal with males throughout her life. You are her guide to how to do that and her testing ground for learning just how males react and to what.

 Question

Do fathers who had sisters do better with daughters?
There is an edge to having witnessed females firsthand, but that does not mean you are at a disadvantage if you did not have sisters. Sometimes a blank slate is best when developing a relationship.

Like any parent, you have your own dreams: Your daughter will play boy's football. Or she'll be an academic star and go to Harvard. Like her mother, you'll need to always assess who she is as compared with what you dream for her to be, and allow her to flourish into her own dreams. Your key is to introduce activities or life choices you may feel she should consider, then embrace those she loves and let go of those she does not. In the end, her happiness should eclipse any disappointment you may have.

The Nearly Traditional Father: The Step-Dad

Once you were an anomaly; now you are easy to find in every crowd. Stepfathers now have more to pattern their behavior on, and more support in the world at large. Depending on when you came into your stepdaughter's life, you'll need to be respectful of her needs and at the same time, working toward building a trustful relationship with her.

If there is a "real dad" involved, it is important you always respect that he is her "real father." Any disagreement you may have with him should be handled only with him, and not through your stepdaughter. If possible, work with your wife, the father, and any partner he may have as a team—agree on all your roles and agree that however your daughter needs each of you, you'll each be adaptable for her and respectful of one another. It can be a tall order, but parents who can achieve this find that the end result—a young woman, who knows how to successfully navigate even potentially stressful relationships—is worth the worry.

The Non-Traditional Dad

Perhaps you are a gay partner with a daughter, or a good friend helping be the father figure in a girl's life. How do non-traditional "Dads" play the right role? First by knowing, and making it known, that you are serving in this role because you love this child and her parent, and you want her to have all the support she needs in life. A positive male influence in a girl's life cannot be a mistake. As long as you work to carve your place in her life in a way that she both is comfortable with and benefits from, you'll be an asset to her in these years.

 Essential

It is important not to take any periods of discomfort or embarrassment the girl in your life may have personally. Rather, work with her to find a way to be comfortable and proud of your role. Give it time.

It might be a good idea to find like situations for you and the girl in your life to role model. A group of friends or even just one other family that is living your same lifestyle can be a great help. And no matter what, always point out to your girl that you love her and want the best for her in life. That's why you are here.

Appropriateness with Her Friends

For years you've been able to pick up and drop off her friends, host play times, and take them all for lunch or a walk at the beach. Now, things are shifting. As girls grow into young women, their perception of all men and actions around all men change. While they once may have thought of you only as Suzie's daddy, now it changes.

Removing the Sexual Undertones

As shocking as it is to see your own daughter develop, it can be disarming to see her friends develop as well. Accepting this gracefully takes care and forethought for a dad. Dads don't want to accidentally wander down that road that Lester did in the film *American Beauty*. Luring and lusting is never okay for a dad around his daughter's friends. You'll want to limit, if not completely avoid, any comments on how girls are growing or how they look. Even the most innocent (from your point of view) comments can be misconstrued. Avoiding them is your best bet.

You will also want to avoid getting too personal with your daughter about her friends. If she wants to talk to you about friendships and issues, that's one thing. If you are the only parent and your daughter needs to talk about this, be sure to let her know it is all in complete confidence and you'll never give a hint to knowing.

Appropriate Attire

Maybe when they were small and her friends were over you'd walk through the house in the short-shorts you wear while doing chores and not much else. If you never stopped it before, you need to stop it now. Cover up around young women; not because you've anything to worry about or be ashamed of, but to avoid any misconstrued reactions or embarrassing moments for your daughter and her friends. Other than at the pool, at least a T-shirt at all times is a good rule. And never, ever, come out of the shower in a towel while friends are hanging out or sleeping over. You may also want to be sure to wear pajama bottoms during sleepovers, even if you usually sleep in the buff. Should an emergency occur, you'll want to be appropriate without having to think about it in the rush of the moment.

Are You Wrapped Around Her Finger?

As much as parents want to mold their children, girls are particularly adept at molding their fathers into beings who are totally wrapped around their cute little fingers. While it's fun to think you'd give the world for your girl (and well you should), it is important to weigh this with what is fair and right.

Signs of Manipulation

It can stroke a dad's ego big time to know that when she needs something fixed, an adolescent girl knows to run straight to Daddy. But this can be a key sign that you are being manipulated. Do you find your daughter coming to you looking for a change in ruling from something Mom has ruled? This most likely means she knows (or hopes) you'll bend and give her what she wants that mom (or the other adult involved) has said no to. Sure, it's tempting to win her love over this way, but is it really good for her in the long run? Most would agree it is not.

If you have found in the past that you've shown a pattern of giving in when Mom does not, you need to address that with your daughter and with Mom there too. Say, "I realize I have done this in the past, but I want you to know that I respect your mother's decisions and will abide by them." At the same time, you'll want your daughter to know she can talk things out with you. In a rare and extremely reasonable case, where you've discussed it with your spouse in private, it's okay to bend. But make sure your child understands why this is an exception rather than a rule, and that your decision was made as a team, not as one parent pitted against the other.

 Alert

Never, ever have disagreements with the other parent about how things should go in front of your daughter. Even if you strongly disagree, present a united front to her and discuss it privately. You cannot expose cracks for her to use to her advantage.

Dad Purchase Power

Starting to feel like an endless well of cash? Teen girls know to take Daddy along when they really want something that's expensive or not on the "necessity list." Since so many dads are at work many hours in a day, they can sometimes try to buy their way into their daughter's hearts. Make sure you are not letting her use you this way. Remember, your attention and love is worth more than every designer skirt out there. Offer her that instead. Spoiling is okay sometimes (that goes for Mom and Dad), but you should never let it replace what is more vital. And don't let your daughter hone in on that and take you to the cleaners. A good idea is to discuss potential purchases with your spouse before diving into them.

Working Toward Your Grown-Up Relationship

Some day down the road, you want to be the father who the daughter always turns to—even later in life. You want her love, respect, and friendship. While this may seem hard to get to at this point, it can be a reality. But today's actions will help you come to that future goal.

R-E-S-P-E-C-T

That is what it means to be, a good dad. In these changing years, you will need to always treat your daughter with respect, and expect the same from her in return. Emotions can get in the way of respect, for both you and her. If you find yourself blowing your top, try to remove yourself from the situation until you are calm. And if she is doing the same, be the adult and remove yourself as well. Don't expect her to act like a grown-up yet. Instead, role model respect for her at all times possible.

 Fact

"I'm sorry" works. You will fall short, and just know that saying "I'm sorry" and addressing the issue head on and honestly helps in the long run. Denial and avoidance do not.

You should also expect your daughter to treat you with respect in public. Nothing is more hurtful and sad to a father than his daughter speaking down to him or rudely to him in front of others (it's hurtful at home; triple the hurt in public).

Make sure your daughter understands how this makes you feel, and if she ever does it, remove yourself—and her—from the situation immediately. She needs to learn to be respectful, even to those she knows will forgive her. (More on such talk in Chapter 4.) And the same goes for you. Speak to her with the respect you expect to receive at all times. Even if she's driving you nuts, keep your cool and don't blow a gasket, particularly in public. If you need an outlet, talk to your spouse or a friend and calm down before talking to your daughter about the situation. Respect demands respect.

 Essential

Things won't always go well with your teen girl, but practice forgiveness. Model for her how to work through a problem and then, eventually, forgive. It's the best lesson you can give her.

Sharing Your Dreams

Nothing works better in solidifying a relationship than sharing your dreams. Make a point of telling your daughter how you envision your future and how she fits into it. "I cannot wait to see what you become in life, and to be there and be proud of whatever you choose" is a good opening. Consider writing your daughter a letter from time to time. There is nothing like putting your thoughts and dreams on paper. She can absorb them at her own pace and even better, treasure them for a lifetime. The written word is a powerful and often overlooked tool in today's world. Sharing via written word could be a moment you two not only build the foundation of your future relationship on, but hold onto as a memory through life.

Eventually, your daughter will move past adolescence, and you probably will be celebrating milestones in life with her. The challenges you are facing right now will make you closer and your long-term relationship stronger. By facing issues head on and working through them with your daughter, you'll be working toward the dream instead of away from it. The more you work at building that strong but realistic foundation today, the better off you'll be in years to come.

Chapter 4

Communicating with Your Daughter

If only it were all as simple as a shared cup of tea, a pat on the back, and the suggestion of a real heart-to-heart. But alas, building and maintaining successful methods of communication with your daughter is a challenge. It's a worthy challenge though, as success here lays the foundation not only for a lifelong bond, but for your daughter's success in life.

Are "Good" Talks a Myth?

You've seen them on television and the movies, and you've heard friends describe them. A teen girl is grappling with an issue, and she knows to sit down and go over it quietly and calmly with her parent. Or a parent senses something is amiss and is able to have a reasonable discussion complete with agreed upon conclusion about it with the teen. Does this really happen in life? Only with incredible insight, great planning, and perhaps a bit of luck.

Modeling Communication for Your Daughter

As parents move toward this era of uncomfortable talks, they will want to look first toward their own relationships and how they communicate there before expecting success with their daughter. Do you and your spouse/significant other or even your own parent communicate in a way that is mature, respectful, and reasonable? In many cases there, the answer is no. Parents who struggle with communication in those areas need to take heed of that old punch line: "I've seen the future, and all I can say is, go back." While you may want to think: *this is my chance to start fresh,* the way your daughter has seen you act and the results (or lack of) she's witnessed may taint her from being open to good communication with you.

 Alert

Of course, you cannot change the past in a snap, but acknowledging past problems, such as a lack of good communication with your own parent, will at least show your daughter that you understand something was amiss and would like to change it.

In the case of communication with a spouse or significant other, if you've been prone to yelling, cutting one another off, or worse, not speaking for hours and even days after a hot issue is discussed, it is now time for you to fix that. Discuss ground rules as parents. Agree never to loudly or visibly disagree in front of the children. At the same time, don't be Pollyanna. Show them that you can compromise and that even if one of you has to compromise, in the end, you both end up happy for the sake of the relationship. Sound too tough to tackle? Then it's not a bad idea to call in the counselor. You'll want to go into these teen years with the rest of your relationship stronger than ever so you can work through this together.

 Essential

It's always important to remind your daughter that relationships are like snowflakes: no two are alike. Yours is unique and requires its own special care. Expectations from her modeled on another girl's with her parents are not good to hold onto.

Understanding Her "Good Talk" Expectations

Chances are, your daughter will be a mix of a jealous girl who thinks some of her other friends' parents are just so easy to talk to and of a girl who'd rather just be left alone. She sways from wanting to be able to share with you (after all, she does love you and deep down needs your support and advice) to being disgusted with even the notion of sharing anything uncomfortable with you. It's up to you to find a middle ground there that not only works for her internally, but works for both of you as she grows.

The first step here goes back to that "Cool Mom" concept discussed in Chapter 2. Your daughter may be under the assumption that some other girls (perhaps most other girls) have relationships with their mothers and fathers that are never strained and always open and helpful. While you cannot "rat out" another mom for perhaps not being as "cool" as your daughter perceives, you can passively show her that strains in communication are the norm. Encourage her to read a magazine article or book chapter that addresses it. Show her that you are not alone.

So she expects you to listen when she needs you to (such as, "Can I have a ride to the mall?" or "Do you have $20?") but be willing not to share when she's uncomfortable or hiding something (such as boyfriend and body issues or problems with friends). It will be key for you to break past these notions early on. While you should not force her to talk, you should try to maintain open lines of communication.

With Mom

In most cases—and it is hard not to lean toward stereotypical here—the mom is more of the rule enforcer and disciplinarian in the family. Girls have communication expectations with their mom, and communication issues as well. It's hard to get a girl to sit down and talk frankly with you if they know you are always going to do what is best for her (who doesn't want to do what is more fun or less painful instead?). Moms will want to do two things: make sure her spouse or significant other shares in discipline duties (and always backs her up!) and always offer up a safe time for communication. Make sure there is a place and time at least weekly, and even more often, where your daughter knows she can dive into some discussion issues if needed. Even if she doesn't have something key to talk about, just talking at all keeps that door open.

Mom's can have their own expectations too. Hey, you were a teen girl once, and you saw and learned a lot. You want to share with her your successes and pratfalls, and help her to be a better person from them. Just don't expect her to really get that you were once that girl. Here, photos and stories can help. Show her who you were; talk about what you did. Show her that you had dreams; some realized, some dashed, and some realigned.

Make yourself a real, live human in her eyes. Somewhere deep down, she might actually realize you weren't always 230 years old.

 Question

What if my daughter barely speaks to me?
Just keep talking to her. No matter how distant or quiet she is, keep communication rolling. Talk about a book, a movie, her school; anything to keep her hearing you and responding in some way.

With Dad

It's easy for a dad to feel out of the loop when it comes to communicating with his girl. Some things are not easy to discuss with the opposite sex, and the stereotype of the dad at the door with a shotgun to meet the date isn't all that old. Today's dads can set patterns with their girls that break that mold. Even if you work often or travel a lot, have a weekly time when it's just you two, talking about nothing or everything. If she pushes back and wants to stop the practice, don't let her. Go out for lunch or a beach walk or whatever you like to do in your town. But do it in a way that you can talk as long as you want.

Dads need to be wary of manipulation though. Girls know they cast a special spell over their fathers, and know how to use it. Be sure in your communication to not make any promises or set new rules that you have not talked over with your spouse.

But dads can have "good talks" with their girls. Share with them the male perspective and respect their privacy when they need it. They will only be the better for it.

When She Speaks Rudely to You

It can sting like you've never felt before, and how you react to rudeness from your daughter is key to helping her evolve into a helpful and functioning adult. As easy as it is to lash back and to be hurt or to jump into denial and pretend it never happened, parents have to deal with it and do the right thing, which falls in the middle of those two extremes.

Hearing It for the First Time

Remember when your daughter was little, and you overheard a teen girl speaking rudely to a parent? You may have actually said, "I'm so glad I did not raise my girl to talk to me that way," to which the mom of any teen would respond to you, "Get back to me on that in seven years." Because it's going to happen. She's going to be rude to you. As many times as parents tell themselves that ahead of time, it's never less hurtful that first time. Some parents compare it to being stabbed with a knife, so deep is the pain. But here's the trick to it all: it's not really all about you.

When you do hear it for the first time, take a deep breath before reacting. Don't lash back. Rather, take your daughter and yourself to a quiet spot and explain to her how unacceptable that behavior is. If you're in a mall, drop what you are shopping for and head to the car. If you are with a group, excuse yourself immediately. Don't let it slide but don't react in front of others. And do not lash back with rudeness. Pattern for her how you can be firm and disappointed and yet still not be rude. This is not always easy.

 Fact

Often, a girl's lashing out with words is her way to work out a frustration that has nothing to do with you. Try not to take it personally.

If and When It Becomes More of a Norm

If rude talk becomes seemingly endless, parents have to take a stand. While some parents believe in letting it roll off their backs (since they know their daughter is just acting out frustrations), the best bet is to deal with it as it happens. Set some ground rules. Make it clear that rude language and treatment is not acceptable, with you or with anyone else. Having set those rules, be ready to enforce them, because an unenforced rule can be worse than no rule at all.

That said, it's not that easy. Parents do have to find that magical place in the sand where they draw the line. If parents were to punish every single time a teen spoke to them rudely, they might not be doing much else. So what's the crossover point? Some might say when the rudeness becomes a verbal assault. If you feel attacked by your child's words—or you witness someone else like a sibling being attacked with words—you must step in.

 Alert

You might want to point out to your teen that under the law, "assault" can be charged and found for menacing words, and that "assault and battery" is words and actions. Some children may not understand that words do truly hurt.

The first action you should take when your child lashes out with rude words is to teach her control. Everyone has moments of rage; it's what you do with them that make you who you are. Try to encourage her to go to her room for some quiet time before speaking more. If she refuses to do this, remove yourself from the situation until she calms down. This could mean going for a walk or a ride in the car. Let some time pass and give her the room to become rational again. It may take time (even years) but your daughter should learn that if she blows her top, her best reaction is some quiet time to let her anger pass before rude words pass her lips.

To Share Your Past (or Not)

When they were little, it was fun to tell stories about your life when you were her size. But at a certain point, you crossed over to a time when your stories might not be all you want your daughter to emulate. Parents of today face a daunting question: should you be honest or hide some facts? The answer depends on how present the information.

Total Honesty?

You smoked pot before school in high school. You lost your virginity to a girl whose name you don't even recall. You got caught drinking and kicked off the softball team. Sure, all those things are moments you are not proud of, yet they are moments that helped shape your vision of life for your daughter. So what of total honesty?

Some parents find that admitting their stumbles helps their daughter see that they are human and that all people make mistakes in life and live to see another day.

 Essential

If you are going to share some of your not-so-smart moments with your daughter, make sure not to glorify them. Help her to see the consequences you faced because of your actions, and why you wish you could go back and change your decisions.

The goal of your honesty should not be to shock or impress your daughter, but rather to help her understand that you really *do* know what she is struggling with. And sometimes, girls who idolize their parents too much (and fear that any misstep would mean not living up to their example) can see that their parents, too, are only human. That can be a conversation starter in itself.

Hiding Some Facts

Other parents don't want to let their child know about mistakes they've made, fearing they might open up the idea of such mistakes to their daughter. They fear hearing things like, "How dare you punish me for drinking when you had 'three-keggers' in the woods when you were my age?" If the truth is you never minded pot and really don't regret using it, you may want to keep that from your daughter at this age. An illegal act is an illegal act, and finding out the brutal truth about that by having to bail a daughter out of jail is not a good option.

Other parents fear losing their child's respect. And in some drastic cases, this could happen. Think through your war stories and ponder over what good it will do your daughter to know them. If the only answer you can come up with is it will shock her, you are better off keeping it to yourself.

Lying: Why She Does It and What It Means

Lies can send a jab of pain through the heart of a parent as swiftly and directly as a knife itself. You try to raise your child to be trustworthy, and you try to show her that so long as she is honest, the two of you can always work things out. Yet girls tend to lie as teens. Why is that? It's a complicated mix of pushing limits and—believe it or not—not wanting to let you down.

She's Testing You

Some lies are like little feelers—put out there to test not only how much she can get away with, but also if you are paying attention and if you have her back. Let's say your daughter has been allowed to walk to the corner playground for a while now, with the understanding that she'll always be with a friend and only go there and back. One day, you drive your car around a corner and see her in a car driving away. When she gets home, you ask her about the playground and she says "It was boring. Same old thing." While she may have been tempted by the car ride and feared you would not let her, she could also be lying to test you.

That's why your best response is to give her a chance to make good. "Are you sure you didn't do anything else or go anywhere else? Because if you did, it is best if you tell me now" is a good response and a chance for her to come clean.

 Fact

Molding the truth to fit your needs is as common as the cold. Don't lose your mind, but don't be accepting of it either. React firmly, but with sensitivity too. She's only human.

If she does come clean with a lie, respond positively, but point out that she cannot lie again because losing trust has its consequence. If she continues to lie, simply say "I know you got in a car and drove away and for now, I can no longer let you go to the playground until I can trust you." You may also want to suggest that, as she grows into wanting to do new activities (beyond the playground, so to say) she should communicate them with you. She might be surprised, with honesty, at what you might trust her to do.

You also need to show her that you have her on your radar screen. It's hard for teen girls to resist temptation and new adventures. By showing her she "cannot get away with the lie," you may help her make a better decision.

Avoiding Disappointment

Some girls lie to avoid disappointing their parents. Particularly with girls who are high achievers, the idea of being merely human in their parent's eyes might be too much to bear. And so, if they "misstep," they look to cover up and lie, rather than disappoint you. It's not easy work to convince said girl that you love her for all she is—faults and glory. Just keep trying. And point out that the disappointment of being lied to is much harder to bear than any mistake she may make. Remind her she's only human.

With girls who are looking not to disappoint, you may want to encourage by example. Show her mistakes you've made recently, and how being honest about them worked out better. Make a deal: as long as she is honest, things will work out. And any time she does lie, always give her the chance to admit it before you accuse her of the lie. "Are you *sure* you were only at the playground? Because if you did go somewhere else without telling me, you can tell me now." Coming clean, really, is as good as telling the truth in the first place, and your reaction will help her gain confidence to be honest next time. With coming clean, there may still be a punishment, but like life in general, she who confesses gains empathy. It is important to note, too, that persistent lying may be a sign of a serious problem, such as substance abuse (more on drugs in Chapter 12).

 Alert

Teens can be like toddlers in some ways, and lying is one of them. Sometimes a teen truly believes if she says something enough, it will eventually be the truth. Maturity means understanding life does not work that way.

Cooling Down Heated Conversations

It can happen from both sides. You start out talking about something seemingly benign, and suddenly you are in a heated disagreement with your daughter. Dousing water rather than gasoline on these situations is your job first, and hers second.

Predicting Abruptions

Your daughter's communication abruptions could be cyclical. Sure, there's the whole hormonal thing, but beyond that, like anyone in life, loss of patience or the ability to communicate well can surround major life moments. Finals, tryouts for a team, prom season, and other similarly intense times are ripe for a girl's ability to reason to fly out the window. It might be a good idea if you, as a parent, heed these scheduled events and use your powers of calm communication even more so during these times. True, there is no excuse for rudeness, lies, or other such things, but showing your daughter that you understand that stress can cause duress may help her deal with it better.

 Question

Isn't the parent always right?
Much as you'd like to believe that, there will be times when you are actually wrong. Admitting it and helping fix the situation shows your own honesty in communication.

You Don't Have to Settle It Now

Remember, anything can be (and probably should be) put off until cooler minds prevail. You'll want to teach this to your daughter by example. Should you find yourselves at each other's throats, take a step back, end the conversation, and pick it up when you can both be rational. Teens don't always like this; they're in a bad mood and want to lash out at you. Refuse to engage. But don't let it go forever. Every conflict must have some kind of resolution, and dropping it while mad and never picking it up again will only teach your daughter denial.

When you do put something aside to cool down, tell your daughter it is not going away and you'll be picking it up as soon as you are both rational. Don't give her the chance to act out more. Rather, coax her into reading or sitting quietly in her room until you can both talk reasonably. Those taking further the heated conversations are the ones you can end up thinking "What were we fighting about in the first place?" That is a waste of time and more scar tissue on a relationship that needs to stay healthy.

Chapter 5

Discipline and Punishments

Remember the days when you could just hang the thought of a visit from Santa or an upcoming beach trip over your young daughter's head in order to nudge her back in line? Discipline and punishment are perhaps the most dreaded—and misunderstood—aspects to parenting an adolescent girl. At an age when you feel they should be wanting (and deserving) more freedom and less boundaries, the truth is quite the opposite. As tough as it is to play "the bad guy," your daughter actually needs you to be just that.

When to Punish and When to Ignore the Issue

Each person has his own level of acceptance, be it for backtalk, rowdy behavior, or just plain acting out. It's important, though, to make sure you set your level not at a place that benefits you as a parent, but a place that benefits your child. It's your job to raise her well and keep her safe, and your own personal comfort comes second to what her needs are at this time.

Clear Ground Rules for All

It is impossible to foresee all the issues you'll need to grapple with your teen girl. Who knows, at the start, if she'll be a homebody or a party girl; an outspoken rebel or a shy child? But ground rules can be set from the start, in a way that arches over most instances you may have to face. Parents should sit down first and discuss their own feelings about ground rules before sharing them with their daughter. Do both agree that if a punishment is threatened and the situation continues, there is no turning back from enforcing it? Are there levels of acceptable punishment you both feel comfortable with? By coming to agreement on these things privately, you'll be able to always show a united front with your daughter.

 Essential

Write down the ground rules. You don't have to hang them in the foyer, but putting these concepts in writing for both parents to agree upon works like a contract of sorts. They do look lovely on the refrigerator. There will not be room for misinterpretation later.

The first ground rule has to be, clear and simply: there can be no such thing as an empty threat. If you say to your daughter, "If this does not stop you will not go to Suzy's party," and then when the act does not stop you still let her go to Suzy's party, you can forget about the impact of your future talks or the respect she might have for you carrying through what you say. This can be difficult for parents. Often, threats will fly out of your mouth that you instantly regret ("Suzy's party is so important to her; now that I'm calm I feel like I really should just let her go. And anyway, I was angry too."). As difficult as it is, once you've thrown down a gauntlet, you, as a parent, need to abide by it, for better or worse. A better idea might be to think carefully about the consequences you offer up. Make sure you have a "bank" of them to draw from that will have meaning for your child but that will not make you feel guilty for a long time.

 Alert

It's not always easy for the punishment to fit the crime, but try to make them. If a child is excessively back-talking, removing Internet access and cell phone usage is a punishment that matches: she'll be forced to only have you to communicate with and work things out.

The second ground rule isn't so simple either: the punishment cannot stand on its own. You'll need to find a time, away from the heat of the moment, to rethink the situation and talk it through with your daughter. What could she have done differently to avoid the punishment? Show her that she had a way out, so that next time she might possibly consider that option. So what if, during this talk, you realize you may have overreacted? It's important to be honest and open with your daughter. Tell her that in hindsight, maybe you could have eased up on her. But also tell her that parenting is not easy, and if you are going to err, it will always be on the side of what is best for her.

When It's Okay to Let It Go

What about the idea of just letting some of this roll off your back? Some parents find this the easy way out in too many cases; others avoid ever doing it for fear of losing their respect (and yes, their power too). Let's say your daughter has had a particularly bad week. She got cut from the high school soccer team, her boyfriend dumped her, and she got excluded from a party she really wanted to go to. Unfortunately, you are the safe place she can vent her anger. While it's not acceptable, in context, it is certainly understandable. It's an old adage: people are kinder to strangers than they are to those they love, and in a way, your daughter's lashing out at you in unacceptable ways at these moments is a sign of her deep love and trust for you. So can you just let it go? No, but you can cut her some slack. Be careful about throwing out ultimatums at this time. They are the ones you truly regret days later.

 *Question*

What about dangerous or illegal acts at unstable times?
No matter what the situation, any act that is dangerous or illegal demands your immediate action and punishment. Your daughter's safety comes first. And you need to show her more healthy ways to work through troubles.

What if you told your daughter she absolutely could not ride in Cindy's car on Saturday, only to find out she did? Mind you, every other kid in town is riding in Cindy's car, but you told your daughter not to. Punishment is needed, but so is further thought. Can you talk reasonably about your concerns with your daughter, and if she has a reasonable response as to why you are wrong, can you change the rule? Absolutely. Compromise is a powerful tool to know how to work in life. By not backing down but then being open to adaptation, you'll once again role model good relationship building for your daughter.

The Enforcer: Mom or Dad?

Here's a thought: How about both? Parents need to show a completely united front in discipline and punishment. This is not always easy to do.

Agree to Disagree (but in Private)

Let's say you feel strongly your daughter's poor grades on a report card demand some kind of harsh action (they were from neglecting homework rather than from struggling in school). You decide that she is off the Internet until midterm (and a check on her grades at that point), and she is only allowed to watch TV after you have reviewed all her assignments each night. Dad, however, feels differently. She needs her social contact via the Internet, and so he disagrees. What's a couple to do? Put simply, you can agree to disagree, but only to each other. And when it comes down to enforcement, the bearing of the message must be almost seamlessly shared between you in the eyes of your daughter. Because there's nothing a girl won't try more than wrapping Daddy around her finger in front of mean old Mom.

 Fact

While more than a majority of moms now work outside of the home, the fact is, our culture still sees Mom as the rule keeper in the house. Dads who love their families will work to change that image and be willing to share that role in a visible way.

The mom is most often the one spouting off the threatened punishment. This is not fun, and yet, it is a necessary task. The emotional relationship between a mother and daughter is intense, and for that reason, can waver from incredibly close to almost hostile. So when a mom is the one doling out the rules and punishments, it can be easy for a girl to think "I wish Dad was here." Moms may want to consider holding off on the doling until Dad gets home and letting him bear some of the heavy lifting needed. The suggestion of this should happen out of earshot and in a place and time your daughter does not catch on. Give her the idea that Dad shares the duty with Mom because he should, not because Mom asked.

Daddy's Little Girl

It was said earlier in the book but it deserves reinforcement here, every dad wants to treat his girl like a princess. The key is to understand that giving her limits and punishments to guide her to being a happy adult is the best gift you can give her. Everyone knows it's empowering for a dad to have his girl come running to him for love and support and protection against "the bad guy," but "the bad guy" can never be the other parent. Look closely at your behavior. Do you tend to coddle your daughter after Mom's been upset or angry? If so, that needs to be put in check. Put your own ego and needs aside. Remind her that as parents, you are a team, and she *is* Daddy's little girl. Just with rules to live by.

No More Time-Out Chair

Finding ways to punish with meaning gets tougher as they grow. Parents have to balance their desires for their daughter to have fun and experience life with what they must allow and not allow in order for her to grow up emotionally and physically healthy. Punishment has to be meaningful to her in order for it to be effective.

Grounding

"You're grounded!!" It's been a parental cry for the ages. Grounding means something different to everyone, but what it should mean is restricting your daughter from activities outside the home for enough time to allow her reflection and ultimately, discussion with you about the issues at hand.

Grounding sometimes comes after a child disregards a preset curfew, or if she takes part in an act you do not allow (such as drinking at a party or sneaking off somewhere). Parents need to remember that grounding puts them in the hot seat too: you cannot just ground a child and then take off for the day or night.

Essential

You may want to work with your spouse on other choices besides grounding. Serving as "prison guard" can be as rough on you as the grounding is on your child.

Grounding today probably also requires removing Internet and cell phone access. Like it our not, our children's main social setting is in cyberspace (see Chapter 13 for more on that). With that link still there, a child may as well be out and about. Do not confuse grounding with just being kept at home. If your daughter is "grounded" but can have three friends over for the night, that's hardly punishment, and definitely not giving her a time to reflect. If you are going to ground, do it all the way. This may also mean keeping her out of her room, if her room looks like Disneyland and is a haven rather than a punishment. Some parents even remove the "good stuff" from rooms, such as TVs, computers, and the like.

Other Options

Denial of meaningful events is always an enticing carrot to dangle in front of a child, but before you do, ask yourself: do you really want her to miss her junior prom because of misbehavior? When weighing a punishment, make sure it fits the crime. You may want to scale back and say "You cannot go to the movies with the gang Friday night" or "I will withhold your allowance for this week." Those can have less impact long term.

Some parents use chores as a punishment. Productive actions, like Tom Sawyer painting the fence, help the child reflect and actually better the world at the same time. This is okay so long as you're not enlisting slave labor. Chores like painting or weeding can actually be therapeutic, like meditation, giving a child time to breathe and reflect on things.

 Alert

Corporal punishment is never an option. Put simply, striking or otherwise physically abusing a child is not only unacceptable, it is illegal. If you feel the urge, remove yourself from the situation before you act out. If you are unable to do this, you need to seek therapy immediately.

When You Should Back Down

Ever feel like you've gone too far? Or that the situation is actually different than you first assumed? Backing down is an option at times, but only with a lot of thought and a good explanation to your child.

When You've Overdone It

Let's say your daughter broke a rule that is near and dear to you, and while it may not have been the worst thing any child has ever done, you went overboard in your reaction and punishment. How can a parent back down without losing respect? It comes down to a well-mixed cocktail of honesty and cooperation. Let's say you threw the dreaded "You cannot go to (major life event inserted here) now!" line. A day later, you're remorseful. Your daughter's crime didn't match that and anyway, missing that event will tint her history forever. After getting agreement from your spouse (and only if you get that agreement), have a formal sit-down with your daughter and talk the situation, including your overreaction, through from beginning to end.

 Fact

Rational discussions and agreed upon conclusions after a blowout can actually teach your child how to work and act in the world in general. This lesson is a good one.

Be sure to point out why you were upset, and what she did to raise your anger. Then, put it on the table. You should not have gone as far as you did, and you want her to attend the event. Can she help you come up with a just punishment that will help her to learn and you to feel like you're getting through to her? You might be surprised at her response. Often, by this point, girls know they've done wrong and actually want to make amends.

When She Has a Point

What if you've laid down a punishment and a day later, your daughter comes to you with a reasonable argument as to why it is unjust? Mind you, if she's just whining "It's not fair!" you can stop the conversation right there. But if she has a good, solid reason why you need to rethink your decision, its vital for you to do so. Think of it this way: not all criminals are made to serve time. You live in a society where admission of guilt coupled with remorse mean something. But, you'll need to make sure your daughter understands one simple thing: the crime can never be repeated again. You also need to point out to her the process you have just gone through with her. You used reason, listening skill and then, in the end, compromise. If she can learn to trust herself to use those skills before committing an unallowed act, she might find herself in the hot seat less often, and you may find less of a need to punish her.

Follow Through

It's so much easier to say than to do. You tell her what the consequences will be, and then she still doesn't back down. Suddenly, you're faced with your own struggle: do you back down or follow through? The answer is key to your success in raising her.

Wish You Never Said It?

Often times, parents will toss out a possible punishment without thinking it through themselves. "If you don't clean your room by 2 P.M. you will *not* go to the dinner party!" What you don't realize is that her not going has a direct impact on you (someone has to stay home to oversee her). So what's a parent to do? The best answer isn't the easiest: you'll need to follow through with your "threat" and live with the consequences yourself too.

And what if the punishment really makes you sad? Let's say your daughter has been back-talking and misbehaving. You've been waiting for her new cousin to be born. But the day before, you say something like "If you speak to me that way again you'll go nowhere for two days!" She speaks that way again, and guess what: you're in a position to keep her from a moment that was going to be truly special. Can you back down? Some might say yes, but consider this: you want to raise a girl who understands responsibility and true consequences. If you carry it through, it might be disappointing, but she'll learn a valuable lesson.

 Essential

Make a list of possible punishments. Write them down and refer to them. By planning ahead, you may avoid blurting out something you'll regret later.

When It's Just Plain Sad

She's misbehaved to the point that you need to restrict her from everything: cell phone, TV, nights out, and yes, this is the week of the big freshman class trip. You gave her every chance to change her ways, and she did not. Feeling bad for her, sadly, is no reason to back down. But that does not mean you cannot feel bad for her. While the event she is missing (and will never happen again) is going on, talk to her. Tell her how disappointed you are that she is not there, and how you hope you can both work together to find a way that this never happens again. And what about bargaining? She might say, "If you let me go to this, I'll stay in two more weekends." It's best to stick to your original punishment. She'll learn: that's life.

Letting Her Face Consequences

The whole point of punishment and discipline is helping to keep our children safe and teaching them to be good human beings. But what if they keep pushing back? Is there a time when you have to just let them face the sometimes-ugly results of their actions? This can be difficult for a parent, who wants the best for their child, to accept.

School Issues

You nag and nag and nag and yet, she does not do all her schoolwork. You take away the Internet and television, and still, you see Fs where there could be easy As or at least Bs on her grade list. How far can a parent go to make an adolescent girl comply to the rules of education? This can be a hard one to swallow, but at a certain point in their teen years, it is no longer up to you. Sure, when she was little you could ask for weekly update of what her homework is and what she has missing, but by high school, it's time for her to make her own choices, and face the consequences. When you consider the pressure of getting into college today and the long-term effect a few poor grades can have, this can be a real hard pill for parents to swallow. But swallow it you must.

This is an example of natural consequences. Parents who are brave enough to sometimes let consequences take their course find their children get a valuable life lesson from it, and without Mom or Dad even having to be "the bad guy."

So you decide she has to find her own way on this one. Don't just let it drop. Explain to her that there will be consequences and "punishments," just not administered by you. Poor grades can mean expulsion from school teams, and in the end, the lack of ability to get into a college. Point that out and let her know: if she wants to change, you are there to support her in any way (tutors, extra help) when she is ready to change her ways. Good grades could mean inclusion in some special events at school—like special trips her class may take. Rewards come for good work, punishment for poor, and it does not take a parent to dole them out.

 Alert

Doing a child's schoolwork for her is never an option. Better to let her fall short than to give her a crutch. It's not about you; it's about her learning that there are consequences for poor work and rewards for good.

Social Issues

And what about things like drinking and sex? (More specifics on these issues in Chapter 11 and 12). Here, a parent's main duty is to keep a child safe. But the child who continues to act out even with all the support a family can muster (including restrictions, counseling and even court intervention), parents may reach a point of desperation.

Fact

A family is not a democracy. Make sure you don't get swayed by the "it's a free world" and "I can do what I want" argument. You are your child's dictator, and for good reason. Democratic families crumble.

You'll want to first work your hardest to keep your daughter from situations where she can make these poor choices. That can be tough, particularly for dual-full-time-working parents. You cannot always be your daughter's keeper, nor can you completely exclude her from any friends she may have made who you believe contribute to her poor decisions. But you can try. If she continues to make bad choices, intensive counseling is needed. If the friendships are hurting things, you may want to consider a school change. And if that does not work, there may come a time you have to say "She will have to learn the hard way." Don't make this decision without help—either from a counselor, the courts or a program like "Tough Love" that helps families to work through such times.

In the end, good discipline and just punishments are a true act of love. It may take years (and even decades) for your daughter to see that, but reminding yourself of it daily can help bring you through this time.

Chapter 6

Your Daughter's Self-Image and Self-Esteem

When it comes to self-image and self-esteem, there cannot be a more challenging time in a girl's life than adolescence. With all the changes she is going through (and never mind the hormones raging through her body), feeling good about who she is both outwardly and inwardly is a daily battle. Parents who understand—at least partially—what is going on in a girl's body and mind can help her steer through these difficult times.

How Self-Image Is Formed

Is there any question that when they were little, your girl thought the world of herself? She was able to strut with confidence in even the most ridiculous of wardrobe choices. She spoke up and loved what she said. She saw herself as fabulous. Then came the early years of adolescence, and all seemed to change. What happened? And what can you do?

Middle School Shifts in Self-Image

According to a Harvard University study, a vast majority of girls experience a shift in their self-image toward the negative in the middle school years, around or at about age twelve. There, the study says, educators see a drastic decrease in self-image and in academic achievement that they don't see in boys. Why? One reason could be simply tied to changes. "Good girls" have by this age internalized a lot of messaging. They must be sweet. They must be thin. They must do well at all things and never cause trouble. With all that internalization smashing up against the external reality (her body is changing; these years can be the "puffy" pre-period years and sometimes even the development as a female scares them; hormones and pressures may cause them to act out as they know "good girls" should not), girls can struggle with how they see themselves versus how they think they must be.

 Alert

The media, as always, plays a huge role during adolescence. Try to find movies, TV shows, and books that show your daughter all kinds of girls: those who struggle, and even fail, but come out fine in the end.

Educationally, things could shift as well. Confused girls back off from schoolwork or struggle more. Slipping from perfect can make them question their worth in their own eyes as well as in yours. It's a good idea to share with your daughter your own doubts and fears at this age. Of course, she doesn't act like you could possibly know *anything*, but your message will sink into her somewhere. Talk about the year you shot up in height and felt gawky, only to find out years later all your short friends were envious. Or if she is slow to develop, point out others you know were too. Let her know that every teen girl's body is as unique as a snowflake, and if she can learn to just adapt to hers as it changes these years, she'll see she's not different from any other girl, because they are all unique.

"You're Special! You're Special!"

Ever notice that today's children seem to get a trophy for everything? Parents—and society to a point—have bent over backward to make every single child on the planet feel like she is special. And she is. But it's important to remember: children are mere humans. They will fail at something, and as life gets more complicated, they won't always be a winner. Driving home the "you are special" message on a daily basis from the day they are born might not be the best way to help your daughter form her self-image. If you've done this up until now, you may just have a child who assumes she is the center of the universe. Narcissism can be the result, with your child thinking all revolves around her and everyone should constantly not just pay her attention, but pay her adoration. Studies have shown that girls who develop into this self-image tend to have shorter personal relationships, are more prone toward aggressiveness, and can be dishonest and overly controlling. This is not what your goal was when you first started telling her she's "special."

Schools and sporting teams can lean toward the "We're all special!" trend too. Cooperative games that all can "win" at the same time; trophies and ribbons even for last place competitors: it all sounds esteem building, but in fact, it's not. What if your daughter could learn that life is about experiences, and that even if she's not given a prize or told "You are special!" she can enjoy life for what it is: a series of ups and downs and challenges, all of which make her personality more complex, richer, and just plain interesting?

 Essential

Sharing your own pratfalls and out and out mistakes at her age can be helpful here. Girls can idolize their parents (even when they are claiming to hate you). Seeing that you are human can strike a chord deep down that says: I don't have to always be the best.

Parents who have long chanted, "You're special," at their daughters need to take a step back from that and learn to be real about who their daughter is and what her place in the world is.

Many employers today complain about entry-level workers who expect too much. They've been coddled and "rewarded" for their every move all life, so when it comes to work, they don't expect to have to work hard or even get a negative (but useful) review. Parents need to keep this in mind—even if their girl is "special."

Competence and Adequacy

SNL character Stuart Smally said it best: "I'm good enough, I'm smart enough and—gosh darn it—people *like* me!" How difficult is it to get a teen girl to adopt that mantra? In her mind, she may fall short often. Helping her understand that sometimes she will and other times she won't will help her adopt a healthy, realistic yet positive mantra of her own.

Competence

Everyone cannot do everything well. But, everyone does some things well. As your daughter makes her way through middle school and high school, it will be crucial for you to remind her of that constantly. Let's say she's not the top student in history. She struggles with the memorization of dates and events. A girl who does well in other subjects may begin to doubt herself as a whole. "If I stink at history, I must be a lousy student" is a frequent reaction. Teachers and parents who notice this might want to help her see that no one (or almost no one) excels in everything. In addition, parents may want to ask her what hinders her in that class, and how she can apply victories in other subjects to this more problematic course.

Competence issues can stretch out past school work as well. From sports (where body changes can change how a girl performs in a sport she has long loved) to social situations, your daughter may question herself regularly. Parents who can help a girl share this dialogue with you or even a sibling rather than internalizing it will find they are able to keep their daughter feeling good about her abilities, even if she stumbles from time to time. This is not easy: most girls do not want to admit they question their own competence. If she can realize that everyone, every age does, that can help.

 Fact

> It is common for girls to slip in areas in the middle school years. Watch closely for cracks and address them as they come up, but always do so compassionately.

Being Honest about Her Abilities

So what if your daughter dreams of winning *American Idol* but her voice is like fingernails on a chalkboard? Parents have a hard time with the idea of dashing a daughter's dreams. After all, her dreams are so much a part of who she is. But a bit of honesty, doled out in a caring and real way, can do a girl better than turning your back to what you know is destined to be failure. By steering her to another activity or by helping her to see this is one she can do for fun but must not expect to be a world leader in, you're helping her understand her competence and put it into perspective.

Parents don't always see their own child clearly. You may see her dancing as world class simply because your love and pride fogs the real picture. But as she passes from the time in her life when she needs to sort out the difference between hobbies and serious pursuits, it's more loving to let her know she needs to face up to her abilities (or lack thereof) and adjust her life accordingly. That doesn't mean she has to quit dancing if she has two left feet. There are dance programs and schools for girls who simply love to dance. Parents who help a girl see that are helping them find a way to do what they love and not feel like a failure. That's a lesson that crosses over to all parts of life.

 Alert

Don't let your own childhood dreams cloud your vision of what your daughter should be. Just because you yearned (and failed) at being a star ice skater doesn't mean you get another chance with her. Let her live her own dreams.

Self-Control and Problem Solving

Does your daughter suddenly seem to have the same reaction to dislikes and problems as she had as a toddler? You are not alone. Adolescent girls often have trouble controlling their rage, anger, and fears. Teaching your daughter self-control and good problem-solving techniques can make these years easier.

Where Rage Comes From

Your day with your daughter has been fine until you ask her nicely to clean her room before going to the movies that night. Suddenly, she's hysterical, screaming not just about her room but about how you treat her, how her home life is, and how she hates school. Where did all that come from? Girls often are unable to let any angst go in public. In school or out with friends, they swallow their anger, worry, and fear so as not to show any self-perceived "weakness." They want to be seen as easygoing, fun, and cooperative. But here is the thing: that anger or worry they swallow does not go away. Rather, it remains bubbling below the surface, just waiting for a chance to get out.

 ## Question

Can I blame her rage on hormones?
No doubt, hormones play a role in teen girl's rage and mood swings. But you cannot "blame" them completely. Hormonal swings will be a fact of her life, and she must learn to deal with them rather than use them as an excuse or crutch.

Rage or anger toward you, in many cases, may not be about you at all. But you, lucky parent, are the person she knows she can let loose on and be forgiven. That does not make it okay though. Helping your daughter calm down and then see where her rage is truly coming from is an excellent tool she can use for a lifetime. But it's not easy to do. The fact that she does not want to admit she has problems (outside of you being an annoying parent), coupled with her deep desire to fit in with her peers can block a girl from seeing what she's really raging about. It may take a day, a week, or a month. But don't give up on helping her learn this lesson.

Teaching Self-Control

She wants a new Juicy sweat suit, and you just plain cannot afford it. Rather than accept that, she goes into full hysterics; screaming, crying, and all but yelling out loud. Didn't all your years of showing her how to control her anger sink in anywhere? It did, but it just needs reinforcement now. The first step toward teaching your daughter self-control sounds simple, but trips up many parents: Don't just give her what she wants to calm her down, no matter how forcefully she protests. Instead, insist that she go to a quiet place until she is ready to talk calmly about the situation: her room, the backyard hammock, wherever she wants, so long as it's a place where she can calm down and reflect. You may have to force her to do this at times. But do.

 Essential

Do you control your own temper? If not, you are setting a bad example for your daughter. Practice what you preach and give yourself a time out from situations until you are ready to be rational about them.

And what about in public and with friends? Your daughter has no doubt seen a friend flip out. Ask her how she felt about seeing that. How did she perceive her friend? Chances are, she'll say it looked immature, bratty, and unacceptable. Remind her that she looks the same way when she acts out in public. Help her to learn to remove herself from the public situation until she can act calmly. This might mean her calling you with a secret code that means you must "insist" on picking her up and taking her home. Once home, let her know she does not need to let the situation go, she just needs to reflect on it, assess it, and decide if it is a situation worth talking about more. How often do you decide, once you've stood back and caught your breath, that a certain fight was not worth having? Of course, such control and insight is difficult for even adults to stick to at all times. But if she at least tries, that's a victory.

Problem Solving

Chances are, your teen girl lacks vital problem-solving skills. This can be for many reasons, the first of which is that you, as a caring parent, may have been "solving" problems for her all along. It's easy to slide from cleaning off a boo-boo and bandaging it to stepping in and fixing a social situation, a problem in school, or a perceived wrongdoing against your daughter. But it's time to step back. Before you step in, arm her with the tools she needs to start solving problems that come along. Tell her to take a deep breath, step back, and study the problem at hand. Exactly what is bothering her? And why did it happen? Once she has addressed that, she can brainstorm solutions. For the first few times, you may want to encourage her to retreat to a private spot and "journal" on this. Writing serves two purposes: it helps her to think it through slowly and it removes her from a volatile situation.

Parents can also help by taking their teen through the problem solving process with projects—planning the family dinner or her school-week wardrobe. She should plan with alternatives in mind. What if the store didn't have Alfredo sauce that week? What if she spilled something on the outfit she had planned on wearing?

Once she has brainstormed solutions (encourage her to put everything down; even ideas that are laughable later), she should decide on a plan of action. If her problem is a teacher who just does not seem to like her or her work, one plan might be to make a point of staying for extra help once a week. Then, it is up to her, not you, to carry out the plan. It is important for her to understand that her actions may not solve the problem, and that not solving it does not mean her effort was a failure or a waste of time. Rather, she should go back, reassess the situation and see if she comes up with other solutions. And in the end, if the problem is not solved, at least she'll know she did all she could to try to make things better, which is a solution in itself.

 Fact

Time can be a solution in itself. By helping your daughter know to step back and assess things, time will tick by and possibly, her perception of the "problem" might adjust, making it not so much of a problem after all.

Coping with Unrealistic Expectations and Rejection

Years of being told she's special and of winning trophies for just about anything may have clouded your daughter's expectations and robbed her of how to deal with rejection (which all people experience at some time). Coping with these issues takes maturity, patience, and understanding. Is your teen up to it?

When Reality Pales to Expectations

She expects to be class president or the captain of her sports team, only to see another teen step into that role. She was a star in her middle school and now suddenly she's just one of a million at her large high school. Girls can be crushed emotionally by expectations that, as unrealistic as they may seem to most adults, seemed like a done deal to her. How do you get a girl to understand that crushed expectations can build character? The first step may be helping her to embrace her realistic expectations ("I will be a doctor when I grow up" or "I will work hard enough in school to get into a decent college") and to adjust her possibly unrealistic expectations ("I will win *America's Top Model*" or "I will date the cutest senior boy in my school"). Helping her to understand that controllable expectations are vital (studies show that girls with positive expectations have lower rates of teen pregnancy and alcohol and drug use), and that unrealistic expectations are wild dreams rather than true goals, is a good way to start.

 Alert

Modern culture's obsession with teen celebrities (AKA "celebritantes") may have skewered your daughter's expectations in life. Help her to understand that Hollywood is not all it seems to be and that teen stars suffer too.

So what if her reality falls drastically short of all she dreamed? If she's reasonable, its time to help her take stock in all that is good in her life. Point out her victories and her wonderful experiences. Show her where she has achieved and impressed, even if she was not Prom Queen or Homecoming Queen. If she can learn to notice her daily victories, the sting of an unrealized expectation might be less painful. It won't go away, but it can be numbed with other victories.

Rejection

She's been turned down by a boy she liked, or she was not chosen for the school talent show finals. Rejection hurts, even for grown-ups. It's impossible and wrong to tell a girl to just let it roll off her back: we all feel hurt and saddened by rejection. But here's a thought to share with her as she deals with whatever rejection has stung her: It's not what you do with your life when all is going well that makes you who you are, it's how you deal with the hard times and rejection that show your character. Easier said than done, and even most adults struggle with that. But present that concept to your daughter and see if it sinks in. Don't insist she buck up and not cry, but do suggest she look at the entire situation. And here's a thought: is she crushed by her own disappointment or the fear of yours? If you built up a chance too much, she may fear she has let you down. Make sure she knows nothing is more important to you than her happiness.

Parents should encourage their daughters to have a good (and private) cry if they are crushed by rejection. But there must come a next step, and it needs to come quickly. Your daughter needs to look at why she was rejected and then, instead of fighting back, figure out if she really needs what she thought she wanted or if, in the end, she's just as well off not getting what she dreamed of. Often, this exercise can open up a new and unexpected door (a new boyfriend she never considered before who is quite nice or another school program she finds is interesting and challenging, for instance). It is said that time heals all, and that might just be the case with some rejections and your daughter. Ask her to reflect and be patient and see what life brings her next. It might just be a great and positive surprise.

 Essential

Honesty is the best policy. If your daughter does not get a part in a play, and you know the other child was better, tell her so, but in a positive way. Then help her find another way to work on the play.

Such mature reaction and reflection is a trait all teens can use, but even most adults don't have. If you can help your daughter do this and help yourself at the same time, you'll be the better for it.

Chapter 7

Developing Emotional Maturity

The process of developing true emotional maturity is one that can, for some people, take a lifetime. It is the lucky person who, during the adolescent years, is given the right advice, role modeling, discussion, and support to grow into a person who can handle upset and loss with the same grace as joy and victory, and who can know when to forgive and move on and when to take action. Helping your daughter with these skills can help her in every aspect of her life.

Helping Her Emotional Maturity Develop

All parents like to say they see signs of it in their children at a very young age: the rare child who seems to know how to share from day one and the little girl who displays empathy. But in fact, development of emotions is a long and tricky process that demands constant support from parents and other adults.

Managing Highs and Lows

Life is a series of highs and lows, but in the adolescent years it seems to swing all the more from one to the other. Parents who teach children that life is never steady, and that good and bad times come and go (and it's what you do with them and how you react to them that makes you who you are) help their child manage emotions. It's tempting in these challenging years to jump in and "make everything all right" for your daughter, but really, that's not helping her to mature. Rather, you need to help her begin the process of managing her highest and lowest moments to the best of her ability.

 Fact

"Magical thinking" is not uncommon in children and even in teens. A child who has successfully (but coincidentally) "wished away" a bad situation may learn to think that wishing is enough. Be careful to keep your daughter's "wishes" based in reality.

Let's say your daughter wins the lead role in a school play. She's in heaven, and you are happy for her and happy to see your sometimes sulky teen jumping for joy. But what if she had not won the part? While celebrating her victory, you'll want to remind her that many other girls were passed by, and that they are still worthy, likable, and good kids. This can send the message that while winning is fun, it's not everything, and that pride does not equate to arrogance. On the other hand, what if your daughter set her heart on the part and did not get it?

Her anger or even depression over that will need to be managed as well. Try to share with her recent disappointments in your own life, like being passed over for a promotion or something else. Show her that trying was a victory, and that sometimes she will win and sometimes she will lose, but she'll always be worthy.

Proper Expression of Joy and Anger

How many adults have you seen gloat over something they really should keep quiet or lash out in anger about something they should deal with privately? This kind of behavior is usually learned and patterned as a child and teen. Your job as a parent is to teach your child when and how to properly express such emotions. The first step is letting them see and know that you feel joy and anger all the time, and find proper ways to display it. Let's take joy first. In the case of the girl winning the play part (or the team part or the school elected position), of course she's thrilled and of course that should show. But there's a fine line between joy and gloating. Teach your daughter to consider the feelings of others as she's joyful. Is her joy in any way at the expense of others? If yes, she'll need to rein it in a bit.

 Alert

Parents need to be careful not to go over the top in their own excitement for their child in certain situations. Life will be full of wins and losses. Celebrate them, but not like it's the biggest she'll ever have or others will ever see.

Anger can be even tougher to show, not show, or control. It's not right to stomp around raving mad every time something upsets you, but neither is it healthy to swallow your anger and never release it. Learning how, when, and why to show anger is truly a challenging task for girls and for adults. The first step toward helping your daughter know how to do this is knowing how to yourself. Do you tend to fly off the handle and yell? Then do expect to see that behavior from your daughter. What if you could learn to use words in a passionate but sensitive way to express your anger about something? What a skill that would be. Try, as your daughter grows, to have her learn to talk through her anger with you. Even if she's inappropriate, at least she's in a safe place where you can hear her out and then help her figure out how and if to express her anger to others. And remember: time heals a lot. While you never want a child to learn to deny true anger, it's a good exercise to learn to put some space and time between what angered them and their eventual reaction.

Aggressive Versus Too Aggressive

No one wants their child to be the passive doormat; nor does anyone want them to be the bully. Yet, developing a good level of acceptable aggressiveness is tricky.

Assertive behavior, aggression's positive counterpart, occurs when children satisfy their needs in a direct and energetic manner while still respecting the rights of others. The need for control and mastery still exists, but it is motivated by the desire to become competent and self-reliant with a competitiveness that is not destructive or hostile. In other words, a girl learns to stand up for what she wants or needs (or deserves) without attacking others in the process or allowing others to feel attacked. This is tricky for girls more so than boys, because society views aggression in girls in a negative way more so than in boys.

 Essential

Your child must learn to keep her aggression under control while at the same time becoming assertive—a balancing act that is difficult to achieve without proper guidance.

Over-assertiveness can become violence. Violence doesn't occur in a vacuum. It involves multiple factors, and feelings of anger, shame, poor self-esteem, and powerlessness underlie violent behaviors. Once violence becomes a coping mechanism, it turns into a habit that is difficult to break. Violence then leads to more violence because the perpetrator feels justified in her behavior as violence becomes a way of life. Any signs of this in your daughter need to be dealt with, and professional help should be used.

But remember: everyone has angry thoughts from time to time but not everyone acts on them. Remember when you talked at home about wanting to make a snarky comment to your mother-in-law but never did it? That's a form of working things out. Encourage your child to use her imagination with you or someone safe, but then to know its nothing she'd ever really do. Sometimes knowing she can just come to you and voice her feelings is enough of an outlet to help make things better.

Coping (and Embracing) Failure

Many girls today, particularly firstborn girls, try to live up to impossible expectations. Be it with grades, in sports, or in other parts of life, they feel they must always win and can never fail. In fact, learning to fail gracefully is a key skill to take through life.

Admitting Failure

Teen girls might not want even to admit failure, and they need to. Parents need to message from the start that failure is a part of life. Everyone who has ever gone out on a limb or stretched her abilities has failed at some time or another. Encourage your daughter to talk about failures and to discuss the situation with someone else. Share stories about the times you've failed, not just at her age but in recent memory. Show her that you can move past failure and still be a successful person. You might want to even use a little humor here. But don't make fun. Be sure to remember that the particular failure is a disappointment to her, so belittling it is not an answer. You may also want to point out to your daughter ways she could have handled the situation differently, like asking for help. You'd be surprised how many girls are afraid to ask for help in failing situations.

Owning Failure

Your daughter needs to own—or accept responsibility for—her failures as well. Let's say she decided to not do her homework in English class. She got an A on every paper she did and test she took, but the five zeroes from not doing homework dragged her grade down to a C-. Some parents today might want to storm the school, meet with the teacher, and find a way out for their daughter so her poor grade does not mar her college transcript. But the reality is, it *is* her grade. Better that you let her see the grade on paper and not get on the honor roll. She needs to feel the consequences of her failure in order to learn from it. This is not always easy for a parent to do.

 Question

What about failures that can mar her forever?
In the case of a legal situation or another failure that could mark her long term, it's okay for a parent to help a child find a way—within in the law—to get a second chance. Our laws are set up to help kids learn from their mistakes. Just don't cover for your child.

It can be particularly hard for a high-achieving girl to admit failures of any kind. This can lead to lying. If you find your "good girl" is lying to you about things, you will need to talk to her about the value of honesty, and the respect one can get from owning up to a failure or mistake. Remind her: it doesn't all magically become okay when she admits failures, but it does show strong character, and that's a win in an otherwise losing situation. In the end, every experience a teen girl has is a learning experience. If she can learn that she will falter but that if she admits it, embraces it, and learns from it, she's really still moving toward being that successful adult she (and you) want her to be, failure can become something she just deals with. If she can learn to fail gracefully, admitting and accepting her mistake and working to make it better, she'll have a skill many adults don't even have.

Stressed Out

There is a lot of stress in the life of a teen girl. First, the physical stresses. Her body is changing daily. Compound on that the exterior stresses: she needs to get into a good college; she needs to decide if she's a jock or a geek; she needs to navigate the social world, and you've got a whole lot weighing down on a girl every day. Coping with stress is key to emotional maturity.

No More Hissy Fits

Wouldn't it be nice to just say that and they'd go away forever? Girls can really go off the deep end over things that might completely surprise you. You're cooking pasta for dinner and suddenly she's screaming about how you didn't ask her if she wants pasta. The anger seems extreme for the situation. This is most likely a case of your daughter using you to relieve her stress. Think of it this way: out in the world and at school, she has to act better. She cannot trust the world to see through any "breakdowns" and still admire her. But you? You are the bearer of unconditional love. That means, if she has to blow off steam, you're the one to do it at. But that does not mean you need, or should, become her punching bag.

Essential

If your daughter seems to lose it over something that confuses you, insist she spend some quiet time in her room or in the yard before addressing you again. Find a "big girl" type of "time out" to help her calm down.

While it may seem silly to you ("I wasn't invited to Susan's party"), the stressors in your daughter's life are more than real to her. Don't ever pooh-pooh them, even if you think they are silly. At the same time, don't feed into it, telling her she should be mad or upset. Rather, work toward helping her let the stress go and then assessing the situation.

You'll need to set that example yourself as well. Learn self-control, and then make an effort to be an example for your daughter to mirror.

Physical Answers

Stress affects bodies. You've felt it: the muscles in your back or neck or even face stiffening up as you stress more and more about things. Girls are no exception. And sometimes, relieving the body stress can lead to helping your daughter relax more about the entire situation. Consider signing up for a parent-child yoga class. Not only will you have a special time together, but she will learn breathing and stretching techniques that you can suggest she use during stressful situations.

Fact

Caffeine can exacerbate stress, and more and more teens are drinking caffeinated beverages each morning and afternoon. Encourage your daughter to stay away from these drinks (and remember, caffeine is in coffee, tea, chocolate, cola, and other places too).

If you see your daughter building up to a stressful moment (studying for a test; hanging up after a bad phone call), encourage her to lay down in a quiet and semi-dark place and breathe in through her nose, out through her mouth. Sometimes, five to ten repetitions of this breathing is enough to begin the calming process. And the breathing is something she can do without being noticed right in the middle of her school or out in a social situation. The outdoors can be a help too. If she's going off the deep end, insist on taking a long walk with her, even if it's just up and down your street. The rhythm of the walking and the breathing will soothe her stresses, and again, she'll learn a life skill for coping with stress. In the end, she has to realize, stress is a part of life. As always, it's what you do with it that matters.

Volunteering and Public Service

Once there were only a few volunteering opportunities for teens. Today's teen world is ripe with more volunteering opportunities than one can imagine, and most, if not all, are excellent ways for girls to develop emotional maturity through responsibility, leadership, and a feeling of success in helping others.

Why Volunteering Helps

This is an easy one: because it's not all about her. Adolescent girls tend to think the world revolves around them and that no one, *no one* has it harder or tougher than they do. Everyone should be working to make sure their lives are better. Getting into a volunteer situation shows a girl that she has much good in her life, and there are others who are more in need of assistance than she is. Volunteering also shows a girl, firsthand, that she can make a positive difference in someone's life and in the world at large. You'd be surprised how many teen girls don't have any idea that they truly can change the world. A good volunteering situation drives that home.

Volunteering means scheduling your time, making a commitment, and following through with it. While your daughter may balk at taking out the trash, she's less likely to blow off the special lunch her volunteer group has planned for foster children in her area. The idea of "letting someone down" becomes clearer in these situations, and in the end, should transfer over to life in general. And then of course there's the practical benefit of volunteering: girls learn job skills they may not be able to in the kind of paying jobs they are given at their age (coordinating a party or helping with the elderly is a big responsibility), and they gain valuable fodder for their college applications. All this is a bonus, but don't push your child to volunteer for those reasons. Just help her see those as a nice byproduct.

How to Know Where to Volunteer

Most schools have volunteer programs your daughter can link into, but there are also opportunities beyond school that she can look into. Find out if there is a particular nonprofit organization she might be interested in. Does she have a good friend who is fighting cancer or diabetes? That could be good motivation to step up and call a local chapter of the American Cancer Society or Juvenile Diabetes Research Foundation to ask if she can be a volunteer. This is a nice way to step into volunteering, and having a personal connection always fuels passion in such programs. Does she feel strongly about the environment? She could find a group that's working to clean the water, or she could help arrange a town-wide clean up day. Has she always loved animals? The local pet shelter may need a hand or even a fundraiser. The possibilities are endless and can easily be tailored to her interests and concerns.

 Fact

A great place for kids to get ideas on volunteering is *www .dosomething.org*. The site, started by actor Andrew Shue, is a central point for many student volunteers.

While it would be nice for your child to find one passion and continue to volunteer for it for a lifetime, it's okay to switch from time to time. Just as adults work to find the right career fit, girls sometimes need to test out different missions to find the one that matches her passion. But don't let her drop a charity in the middle of a needy time. If she stepped up to run the local diabetes walk, she needs to see it through. Once that task is done, it's okay to move on if she's found another cause she feels passionately about. Volunteer jobs, because they mean so much to so many, can even teach responsibility more than a paying job. Conscience weighs in, and your girl learns a valuable lesson from it—another step toward emotional maturity.

Learning on Her Own

Learning on her own is as much about you as it is about her. A time comes when you must let your daughter sink or swim. This can often be more challenging for the parent than for the child, but it's a necessity on the road toward emotional maturity.

It's Not Your Life

From doing homework for them to picking up pieces of a disaster to covering up for them in a bad situation, many parents try to erase their own errors via their daughter. But guess what? Confronting those mistakes made you the adult you are. This is a hard process for parents who have intervened from the start, but it is one you must undertake.

Let's say your daughter's so-called friends suddenly turn on her one day and are hurtful to her. Your parental instinct wants to stomp down to the mall or the schoolyard and set them all straight. However, your daughter is not a toddler anymore, and you can no longer step in the middle of issues with friends.

Alert

If physical violence is a possibility, you need to show your daughter how to seek help through her school or the police. Do not try to address issues of violence on your own.

The idea of trying to take teen girl issues to another teen girl's parents never ends well. The issues are up to the girls to work out, and the parents will only end with hard feelings amongst themselves—possibly holding grudges well past the time the teens work things out. It's okay to give your daughter advice, but you cannot be the facilitator of the situation.

When the Mistake Is Costly

It's hard to accept that your child needs to face consequences for her actions, but she does. If you find your child in this situation, your best bet is to let the chips fall, but hold her hand all the way. Let her know that despite her mistake and impending punishment, there will be a new day, and throughout it, you will love and respect her. The girl who can cower behind her parents and get away with her infraction is the girl who learns she can sneak her way through life and always have someone to bail her out. The girl who holds her head high and accepts her punishment is the girl who learns from it, and hopefully, does not repeat her digression. Which girl would you rather have raised?

Chapter 8

Miss Independent

Your goal in raising a child is bringing her to a point where she is able to cope—and thrive—on her own two feet. With girls, the process of moving toward true independence is a long, complicated dance. As you begin to give her a taste of freedom and free will, you'll take one step forward and sometimes, one step back. Knowing when and how to allow your child independence is complicated and necessary in her journey of personal growth.

Age-Appropriate Independence Goals

From the time you take your child home from the hospital, you are pushing her toward independence. She can sit on her own! She's taking her first steps! Now she can write her own name! Come the adolescent years, the "firsts" are just as thrilling but more complicated. Parents need to decide carefully when to push and when to hold back as their daughters grow into independence.

"She's Very Advanced"

Admit it. As a parent, you like to think your daughter is more advanced, more trustworthy, and more mature than the average girl. And maybe she is. But even the most mature and trusted child should not be thrust into situations that she simply is not ready for. Today's parents seem more and more to lean toward pushing independence as a sign their daughter is "advanced." But do freedom and intelligence really coincide? Only to a point. Let's say, for instance, your daughter is trustworthy and has never (in your knowledge) gone against your will or wishes. She's twelve, and she now wants to be able to walk to the downtown ice cream stand that you've always driven her to. You've seen some of the older girls walking there and hanging around, and in your heart, you'd like your daughter to be accepted by these "cool" and older girls. Should you let her go? The answer should lie in her personal safety and in what other kids her age should be doing, not in her being "exceptional" and in you wanting the older girls to like her.

 Fact

Even the smartest girls can make poor decisions. Just because your daughter has always done the right thing does not mean you should open up risky situations to her. As one parent puts it, "She's a good girl, but why hand her a loaded gun?"

You'll want to err on the side of safety. A younger girl might not be ready to face certain issues that pop up when she hangs out with older girls, and might not be totally secure in walking to a place she's always been driven to. But that doesn't mean you'd need to walk her into the ice cream store holding her hand. Take small steps. Offer to drive her there with a friend and drop her off. Tell her she must stay there until you pick her up at a specific time (after a short while). Baby steps like this can help ease her into independent situations.

 Essential

When you do hold your daughter back from a freedom, explain to her why, and let her know that there will be a time in the future you do allow her that freedom. Even if she complains, she'll know you are thinking it through.

"She Seems So Mature"

Some girls seem to grow up fast; they walk early, they excel in school, or they start reading more advanced books and magazines and talk about boys and social situations at a young age. Is this a signal you should allow your daughter to move toward more independent situations? Absolutely not. As mature and "in touch" as your daughter may seem, it's up to you to keep that in check; to only move her toward what any girl her age would be ready for, even if she pushes you to do otherwise. It is important for parents to remember that some of the "mature" traits your daughter may be showing could be just that—show. She may be trying to convince you, and more importantly her social world, that she's all grown-up, when in fact, she's still a child who needs structure, guidance, and rules to live by. It's a challenge for parents to hold these girls back, because they'll fight that they want to be free. But it is, in almost every case, what is best for your girl.

So what are appropriate ages for independence goals? Girls seem to want the same things first: a trip to the movies in a large group of girls and without Mom and Dad along is a good first. Many parents allow this to begin in middle school, with some supervision. Girls can be dropped off at the door of the theater and picked up there immediately after the movie lets out. (Don't fall for the "drop us off at the mall door" trick. Today's malls are rife with trouble. Any parent who walks through one on a Friday night can see what complications could meet a girl wandering the mall alone or with a few friends at that age.) Another step at the younger range of middle school is letting her ride a bike to a nearby friend's house. Sure, you did it as a kid, but today's world is more complex. Setting up a plan—she'll leave your house and take the route you've shown her by car and call you immediately when she arrives—can feel like true freedom to a younger girl.

 Alert

Cell phones have allowed parents to feel more secure letting their girls roam free, but remember, she can tell you she's somewhere she really is not. Don't rely completely on a cell call. Back it up by talking to a parent who is in charge on the other end.

For an older girl, you'll need to decide when it's time to let her be alone with boys and go on dates, as well as drive in cars with other teens. Dating is covered in detail in Chapter 11, but as it pertains to independence, it's safe to say a girl is not ready to be on an alone date with a boy until she enters high school. Do you see more and more middle school girls on dates? Of course. But just assume their parents are those "Cool Moms or Dads" you should not be. However, you may want to consider letting your daughter take part in coed group activities, like movies or bowling or a beach trip in your seaside town, when she is in seventh and eighth grade. Try to stress that she needs to learn to be friends with boys, and always make sure she is in a supervised situation. If a friend is having boys and girls over her house, talk to the parents and make sure they will keep an eye on them the entire time. Dark basements are not a good place for your young girl when she first hangs out with boys.

When to Let Go and Of What

Of course, there will come a time when you have to actually let go and trust her on her own. But when? And how? It all comes down to tiny steps toward freedom that she takes with you watching over her.

Checking Up on Plans

For whatever reason, girls despise your checking up on their plans. Every time you dial a phone to talk to the mother on the other end of the plans ("We are all going to Bobby's house and yes, his mom will be there"), be ready for the "No one else's parents check up on them like that!" screech from your daughter. As much as your daughter hates this, it's a true act of love and, until your daughter is of legal age to make her own decisions (eighteen for most things), it's your duty to check and make sure she has the right supervision at all times. Don't be surprised if the parent you call tells you that you are the *only* parent to have called; that doesn't mean you were not correct in doing it. And if your daughter complains that you are the only parent who called, tell her that's because you care, and it's not going to change. Making sure things are as you want them to be is an act of love for your child, even if she does not see it that way.

 *Question*

What if the parent in charge does not seem trustworthy?
Then you need to keep your daughter home. She'll tell you everyone else is going, and they may just be. But it's your job to care for her well-being, not any other child's. File it under "cruel to be kind."

It is okay, too, to make sure what your daughter claims to be doing is actually happening. Checking movie times (both start and end) may feel to her like you don't trust her, but really, you are setting safe limits for her. As she gets older and she's done these things many times, you'll move to a time when you don't have to check on little things, like movie times. Be sure to point this out to her. While you are still calling parents and checking on things, or not allowing her to drink alcohol even if other parents do allow it (see Chapter 12 for more on this), you can point out to her that she is gaining freedom and spreading her wings, even if it's not as quickly as she'd like.

When Loose Plans Can Be Okay

"Mom, I'm sleeping over Ellie's house tonight." "What are your plans while over there?" "I don't know. Whatever." You've heard it before, and for years, you've called the other mother or father to discuss what they allow their child to do and what your rules are. But is there a time when you can just trust your girl to go? In time, indeed there is. The first step is getting to know the other families and girls she hangs around with. You'll see patterns: some girls have rules like your child's, while other parents seem to never know where their children are or what they are doing. Even in the case of a most responsible girl, you'll want to keep tabs on her in the latter situation. But there should come a time, with experience and years, that you can just say, "Go and have fun!" This can happen after you've had many discussions about what you expect from your child and what your rules are. When you do, just let her go, and to compliment her: "I'm so proud that you've come to a point where I can trust you like this."

 Fact

Girls will stumble. If they do get freedom and then mess up, take a giant step backward and work with her to win it back again. When it comes to her safety and well-being, it's one strike and you're out.

There may also be some activities that you, as a parent, are more comfortable letting her do. You hate the mall scene, but you don't mind the cybercafé in your town at all. If she asks for something you are not comfortable with, offer up some other options. She may dig her heels in and just stay home, but at least she will see that you are open to some forms of freedom for her. And remind her that the more positive experiences you have with small freedoms for her, the more you'll move toward letting her have complete independence. Remember: more than a few girls who have hated their moms for saying "no" have thanked them a week later when they realized the scene they wanted to head to was not a good one.

What Not to Let Go Of

As sophisticated and smart as your girl might be, you must hold tight to certain restrictions. Don't put her in a sexually charged situation, like a coed sleepover (more on that in Chapter 11). No matter what others are doing or what your daughter may claim, minor girls do not belong in any kind of intimate situation with boys. The same goes for alcohol. Today parents may say "I'm watching them and they cannot drive anywhere anyway," but the fact is, underage drinking is illegal and unsafe. Insist she stay away from these activities during her high school years. Do not fall prey to the parents who feel that teen girls should experience all this so they can handle it. And don't listen when your daughter complains that "all the other kids can do it." What matters are your rules, and for now, your rules say "no" to such things. The time will come. But it's not now.

Too Much, Too Soon?

Every parent wants their child to have everything first. Be it material or social, parents want their girls to have everything they did not as a child, times three. But parents need to take pause: too much too soon can be harmful to a girl's emotional and even physical development.

Social Aspects

Remember when you could plan a tea party for a birthday or a craft day for playgroup and all was well? It's all changed so much now. Your girl sees what's going on around her, in her real life and in the media, and she wants to hop on board. Today's girls push for more social advancement more than girls ever did before. From the above-mentioned coed sleepovers, to dating, to what time curfew should be, today's girls want more than they truly can handle. And some parents, for fear their girl won't be "popular," give in to what they feel the rest of the parents are allowing. Here's an idea: if all parents tried to stick to rules that are reasonable and safe, all girls would not feel the need to push for more.

 Essential

Host a coffee or potluck dinner with your daughter's friends' parents and try to come to a group agreement on things like curfews, party rules, and expectations. If most of you agree, your lives will be easier. For a while.

Your daughter is going to be assaulted by social images. Think Lindsay Lohan in a bar as a teen, or the Olsen twins out clubbing as young girls. It's your job to show your daughter why that is not right, and why you're holding her back from things like under twenty-one nightclubs (until she's eighteen anyway) and heading out to concerts in limos without adult supervision. Sure, she'll say everyone else is doing it, but you don't care about everyone else. Remind her: the time will come for her to do such things and when it does, it will all be exciting to her, instead of old and boring.

And what of middle school semi-formals and dinner dances? Parents should consider working against such "grown-up" events that set the stage for more "grown-up" activities. It is just as easy to plan a field day, with games, food, and music. Try to keep their social events age appropriate, even if it means pushing back against some other parents. And if you can show your daughter and all the other kids her age that fun can be age-appropriate, you'll be doing everyone—not just your own child—a favor.

Emotional Aspects

It's the plain truth: as smart and kind as your teen daughter might be, she is not mature enough to handle some independent situations she may find herself in if you allow her too much freedom too soon. Let's say you allow her, as a high school freshman, to go on a one-on-one date in a car with a senior boy. You like the boy and trust him, and you know your daughter has good morals. But leave them alone in a car and she may begin to feel pressure that she is not ready to deal with. She may act a way she's not wanting to for fear of rejection; she may take part in something she does not believe in just to be accepted by an older, cooler crowd. Parents can help a girl avoid that by waiting to allow her to be in such a situation until she's worked her way up via boy-girl group events, dates with boys her own age, and lots and lots of talking with you (even if she resents it). Put aside your pride at her being asked out by the hot older boy and put forward instead her own emotional and physical need to be protected. The time will come. Too much, too soon can never be taken back, and if you do let her have too much freedom too soon, she could regret it for a lifetime. Slow and steady.

Learning to Let Her Survive on Her Own

There will come a time when you do need to let go a bit. The year before college is a year of transitions, and while you may not be ready, it's time to begin to trust. So long as she is safe and making relatively good decisions, this will be the time to see if you've helped her grow up responsible enough for independence.

Giant Steps Toward Independence

It strikes you when you mail that first college application out, or when you first realize she'll soon be eighteen—old enough to serve her country if she so chooses. With all your holding back and watching over, it's time to let her begin to be free. This can be hard for parents. After all, seventeen-year-old girls, for the most part, are far from fully mature. But if you've done your job, it's time to set her a bit free and—if necessary—to let her learn from her own mistakes.

Let's say your daughter wants to go to a big nearby city with friends for the day and come home long after dinner. She's been there with you many times over the years, and she has a plan. This is the time to let her go. Encourage her to be safe: park in a good garage or use public transportation; don't meet up with strangers and stay in the safe parts of the city. Beyond that, though, let her go.

 Alert

Develop a code word for bail out. Ask your daughter to call you at a certain time during the night during any activity. If she says the code word, that's your signal to insist she must come home. She'll fight you for show, but thank you when she gets home safe from the bad situation.

Another situation might be an all-night event, such as the prom. Kids like to stay out all night for these major events, and she's at an age now where, in the right situation, you can trust her. It's still smart to talk to the parents who are hosting the kids, but let your daughter know she's earned the right to go, and then trust her. An uneventful night will be reason to celebrate her maturity, and a troubled night (such as being caught drinking) will be reason to let her face her punishment as a near adult. After all, that is what she is now.

Consequences
So what if she is given a freedom and does something wrong? Most parents agree that rules are in place for a reason—

that is until their own children have to face the consequences of them. Let's say your daughter is a star tennis player. Her senior year play will be crucial to her getting a tennis scholarship. But a month before, she gets caught drinking at a school event. The rules state she is to be suspended from school and kicked off sports for the remainder of the year. Do you go to the school board and fight it or let the chips fall? The strong parent chooses the latter. Your child knew the rules and chose to abuse her freedom. Facing consequences, no matter how harsh they may be, is the only real choice for helping her grow into a responsible adult. Parents need to accept this for the sake of the young adult they are raising.

Money Issues and Teens: What's Realistic?

Learning to be independent also means finding ways to be financially independent from parents. To do this without harming other parts of a teen's life in this world of $10 movie tickets, $3 a gallon gas, and $150 jeans can be a struggle. Parents need to find a way to teach financial independence and still support children at the same time.

Allowances

It started as a few bucks a week for candy or whatever, but the allowance issue has ballooned into a nightmare. Your daughter wants more things and to do more things, and it's all expensive. How much do you give her and for what is up to you. But one thing is for sure: she needs to learn that you are not a bottomless wallet and that, indeed, money does not grow on trees. It's a good idea to set a reasonable allowance based on what her needs might be. A movie on Friday could mean $15 to $20 each week; a soda here and there all week another $5 or so. And she'd like a bit of discretionary money to save for something big or spend as she wishes. Sit down with her and figure out the average week, then balance it with what you can afford as a parent. Then, attach some responsibilities to the allowance, such as cleaning her room each Thursday, emptying the dishwasher, or mowing the lawn, whatever you agree she can do. Then stick to it. If she does not do her work, she will not be paid. Just like the real world, almost.

 Essential

What about paying for grades? Some parents swear by it, but others feel the reward for good grades should come from within. It's a good idea, if you don't pay for grades, to explain that to your child.

What if your child runs out of money before the week is over and her friends are doing something she wants to do? Just once, you may want to give a bonus or advance, but don't make it a habit. She needs to learn to plan her spending and live within her—and your family's—means.

This can be a valuable lesson when it comes to expensive items. Let's say she lusts for a pair of $200 jeans. You tell her she can save her earned money and buy them. She does it, and then she cannot afford to go anywhere in them. Rather than give her the money, let her feel the repercussions of her decision. Next time, the on-sale jeans might just look cuter after all.

Credit Cards

More and more kids have credit cards now. Do you want your child to have one? Most adults know the lure a credit card can have. You don't have to think about what you are spending until that bill comes in, and purchase decisions made can be rash and even bad. Even if you have the means to pay any balance every month, it is a better idea to teach your child what money really means. Try this: when you go back to school shopping, instead of just purchasing each item as your daughter chooses it, hand her an amount of cash totaling the amount you want to spend. Tell her it's hers to spend on whatever she needs for back to school. Watch as she suddenly thinks twice about the ultra-expensive jeans and realizes she can buy three pairs of another brand for the same price. Real money leads to real decisions. Credit cards can rob girls of that important lesson.

 Alert

More and more credit card companies are soliciting teens for their business. Warn your teen *never* to fill out an application form, even if it's for a free gift or a one-time discount.

With the easy access to credit through in-store sign-ons and other solicitations, more and more teens are getting deep into debt, sometimes without their parents even realizing it. (How many times have you been told "You can save 15 percent today!" by a salesperson; your teen probably has been too.) This is a danger for many reasons. First, the teen has to pay off the debt, often needing to work more and more hours (and that takes away from school and extracurricular time) and second because this debt can harm her credit score for a good long time. Sit down with your daughter and explain to her what a credit score is and how it can hurt her future. If she must have a credit card, give her one that is attached to your account, and help manage it for her. Give her a very low limit and sit down and help her pay it each month. That way she can feel grown-up, build credit, and learn responsibility all at the same time.

Her First Job

So she decides she wants a job. In a way, you are proud of her willingness to work hard, but it is important here to remember she has a job already: it's called school and learning about life. If your child is doing relatively well in school and socially, a job with a few hours that does not get in the way of school and fun is acceptable from fifteen years old on. But if her job starts to get in the way of school and life, it's time to back off, no matter how much she likes that extra cash. If she insists on having a job, tie her permission to work to how she maintains her schoolwork. If it slips, she must cut back on work hours or quit completely. And help her look for a job that will not stress her out too much. Retail is a common choice for young women, but other choices are good too. If your town has a business that is owned by a family (who has children of their own and understands the need to schedule kids carefully), that's always a good choice.

 Fact

Work teaches responsibility, and helps a girl feel she can pay her own way and learn that money is a tool. Work also builds character.

In the end, your child's first responsibility is to get a good education. Work should never interfere with that, and work should never be unsafe for your child. Federal and state child labor laws restrict where your child can work, what she can do, and how many hours she can work. Laws vary in each state, but none allow children to work under the age of fourteen. Some states do not allow teens under sixteen to operate deli slicers, and some do not allow children under eighteen to work past 10 P.M. on school nights.

Her First Car

The same can be said for a car. Kids who buy cars find themselves slaves to the costs immediately: the costs of insurance, gas, and maintenance can all force a kid to have to work countless hours. So while your daughter may feel buying her own car is a sign of independence, it can actually make her a slave (more on driving in Chapter 7). As much as she may fight you, try to hold off letting her buy a car and taking on too difficult a job. You know—even if she doesn't—that she has the rest of her life for bills and work. Many high schools warn parents at freshman orientation about "car-itis," a syndrome that strikes teens who purchase cars. Their parents are proud when their child saves the money for the down payment, but in time, the child ends up working long hours and struggling to keep up with insurance and even gas bills. This is a time for learning and growth, not for struggling with bills. Just doing her schoolwork, being part of a team, and working toward growing up is all she needs on her plate.

Chapter 9

Your Daughter's
Value System

You've thought and said it many times in your daughter's life, even when she was a tiny newborn. Of all the things you wish for her: intelligence, school success, solid friendships, and a happy career, the one thing you crave the most is for her to be a *good person*. As much as you work to establish a value system from the time she walks, it is in the adolescent years that it gets put to the test and, in the end, is formed for life.

The Importance of Character

Everyone knows someone who's a smashing success at something—she's either a millionaire CEO or a stage star or the like—and yet, she seems to be missing something key. That key is a strong sense of what is right, otherwise known as good character.

Building It from a Young Age

A good sense of self and character is the core of what makes up a good adult. For adolescent girls, those who are able to build and hold onto a strong sense of character from an early point survive these dicey years more intact than others. Think about it: it is your character, or your true vision of who you believe yourself to be, that is at the base of every decision and every reaction. Let's say your child, deep down, has a strong sense of always doing what she sees as "right." Even if she acts in a way that her base character would not find appropriate, she's going to feel remorse. And sometimes, with teen girls, remorse is the best you can hope for. After all—everyone stumbles. It's what you do with that stumble and how you learn from it that shows who you really are. Good character helps with that.

 Fact

Girls who participate in leadership programs and roles, such as student council or scouting, are given more of a chance to explore and build strong character qualities.

So in the early years, you feel proud of your daughter's character. At playgroup, she stands up to the preschool bully and reaches out with kindness to the girl whom no one seems to want to play with. In her early school years, she shows leadership, speaking up in class and offering to sit next to the new kid in class. But around the start of fifth grade, things seem to change a bit. She might side with some other girls being mean to a girl. Or she holds back from being a leader in class. Where, you wonder, have you gone wrong? In fact, you have not.

This is the time in life when a girl begins to feel pressure. School gets tougher, homework is longer and harder, and she may now have a series of teachers instead of just one to focus on. In sports, the "everyone plays" rules begin to change and in some cases, girls may be cut and experience failure. All this, plus the change to a middle school, can weigh heavy on a girl and make her question or play with her character.

Alert

If your daughter is cut from a sport she long loved and considered part of who she is, work hard to find another sport or activity for her to relate to and excel in. And work with the other mothers to keep your daughter in the friendship loop of the former teammates.

The child who works through these times and is able to stick to the core character beliefs you've tried to instill since she was young (and you saw in play in those playgroup and early school years) is the girl who will get through adolescence with a strong, quality character intact. It's not easy, and there will be times even your adult character questions what is right and wrong. But the ability to stay strong and focused on her personal beliefs is a gift to a teen girl.

How Parents' Character Plays a Role

First, "what is right" is, in the end, a personal decision for every person to make. There are basic "rights and wrongs," such as honesty, kindness to others, avoiding things like stealing and physical harm to others, and caring for others. But beyond that, it's up to you. Some people believe that so long as you are a "success" (in other words, as long as you make a lot of money or rise to the top of a company or have a special sports skill), then you are all you need to be. Stepping on others and looking out for your own end goal comes first. Others believe that, before any of that can matter, you must be a caring person who helps others. As you work to help your daughter develop her character, it is a good time to reflect on your own. Do you "practice what you preach?" Are you the person you want your child to be? If the answer is no, all is not lost. It's never too late to better yourself.

 Essential

Be an adult volunteer in a way that is visible to your child. Choose a charity—or even your child's school—and get involved just for the sake of helping the world. It will send a message to your child and help your own character as well.

The challenge for some parents here is that wanting to get the "best" for your child can overshadow your ability to show strong character. Let's say your daughter is a pretty good soccer player and is on a youth team that does relatively well but does not win the league. Two girls on the youth team are not strong players, but the league rules say no one can be cut at this age. Do you teach your child that playing for the sake of playing is what is right at this age? Or do you complain about the two girls who are "holding the team back?" It's hard to put what is right ahead of what might be advantageous for you child, but if you can do so, you'll give your daughter a tool more valuable in life than any soccer skill can ever give her. It's a challenge, to be sure, particularly when you watch all the other "soccer parents" around you. But doing the right thing will pay off in the long run.

Affection and Kindness

No parent wants his or her girl to be a mean girl. Parents want their girl to grow up understanding that kindness to all is key, and that affection, used properly, is never something to shy away from or hide. In the teen years, all that can be difficult to make work, at least to the outside world.

Be Kind to Friends (and Family)

It's such a simple thing to say, and yet many people often find it complicated to do. *Be kind.* How many times have you said it as your daughter grew? When she was in those toddler years and wanted to grab a toy from another playmate, you drove home the message: don't be mean. As she worked her way through the early school years, you reinforced it with songs about kindness, stories about what happens when someone is mean, and examples of how she can show her kindness to others. You clucked your tongue at older girls you saw being mean to others, and particularly those who lashed out at their mothers. You may have even seen a teen girl talk in a mean voice to her parent and thought, "I'm glad I didn't raise my daughter that way!"

 *Question*

Is it possible for a teen girl to avoid ever being mean?
Probably not. Think about your own life: you snap at times. Teens have more pressure on them and will snap. But learning to make good is as important as trying to be kind. Don't expect perfection, but do expect remorse.

It seems easy to say that kindness should begin at home, but with adolescent girls, home can be the toughest place to be kind. The girl who long played nicely with her siblings and cuddled up to Mom and Dad in the evening suddenly begins lashing out at you. In a way, consider it a compliment. Girls at this age have a lot of pent up stress and anger. They need to find a place they can channel it where they know they are safe. You, dear parent (who she knows deep down will love her through eternity for better or worse), might just be the safest place to vent that anger. But does that make it okay? No. But at least know as it is happening, it is because she loves you.

While you can understand why your child is lashing out at you and at siblings, you cannot simply allow it to become part of life. Don't lash back, but do find a way to show your daughter that she needs to treat everyone—even those who will forgive her quickly—with kindness. When she lashes out, ask her to go to her room or a quiet place and calm down. If she continues, remove yourself (or the sibling) from the situation. And when she is finally calm, talk it through and ask her to apologize. Make her understand her lack of kindness hurt. And show her that apology—and the other person's willingness to forgive—is an important part of kindness. When she does get the nerve to say sorry, your instant acceptance will be a valuable lesson that wounds can be healed and that wrongs can be made right, all in the name of kindness and character.

 Alert

Check your own temper when a child lashes out at you. Yelling back will only teach her to yell more. Stay calm, and if you cannot, remove yourself from the situation until you can.

Be Kind to Strangers

Everyone wants her child to be open, friendly, and kind. But things can get in the way. Shyness is one of them, as well as exclusionary behavior learned by friends and even family. How do you get your child to be open to others and still keep to herself as much as she'd like?

For shy girls, this can be a huge challenge. Shyness is often misinterpreted as snobbery. A child who is shy may have trouble even saying "hello" to someone she does not know. Let's say you are at the store with your young, shy daughter. You bump into a friend you know who has not met your child before. You introduce them, and your daughter turns her head the other way, avoiding saying "hello" and even making eye contact. In your heart, you feel for her shy self. But the best thing you can do is encourage her, from a young age, to work past her shyness and give back at least the minimum acceptable response. In this case, a simple "Hello, nice to meet you," would do. Sure, she's not going to chat on and on, but she's shown a simple kindness.

 Fact

Extreme shyness can be pathological. If you notice your child is completely unable to interact with others, talk to her health care provider about possible surrounding issues. There may be an underlying physical or emotional issue at work here.

But what if your daughter, as she grows, just seems to be a snob of sorts? It can happen. First, you need to look at your own patterning. Do you socialize exclusively with one crowd and really have no use for others outside of that crowd? If you are, don't think your child does not notice. Do you tend to socialize with people who live in the same type of houses as you or have the same background? Again, you are patterning for your child. Girls can fall into cliques from an early age (some kindergarten teachers have even noticed them forming at that stage and worked to break them up). The more you can teach your daughter to be kind to all and accept all kinds of friendship possibilities, the better a character you are helping her to form.

Essential

You must intervene when you witness your child committing unkind acts. Consider any mean or cruel act as a punishable offense and don't let it slip by. Not only will you teach your child to act better, you may teach her to stand up when others act badly as well.

Ask your teen to consider this: even if she does not make someone her best friend, there is no reason not to be kind to another person. Ask her to think about what she feels when she sees friends being mean to others. Sure, she'll say she wants to avoid being the one under attack—but why? If she can understand that unkind acts are truly hurtful to others (the same, truly, as reaching out and slapping someone), perhaps she can learn not to take part in them. The rare teen girl will adopt this to the point of sticking up for others. That is true character. At no age is acceptance by "cool kids" more vital than during these years. If your child can see past that and choose simply to be kind, you're on your way to success.

Showing Appropriate Affection

Remember when hugs weren't at a premium? In fact, restraint in this area is not exactly a bad thing. You really don't want a teen girl walking around hugging everyone she sees. But still, you think, does she have to stiffen up like a board every time someone who cares about her shows any kind of affection? Here, the old adage is so true: children live what they learn. Are you not really an outwardly affectionate person? Do you dislike that about yourself? Your teen child offers you a chance to change that. You might want to initiate a conversation. ("Have you ever noticed how John's family always hugs one another hello and goodbye? I always wished my parents would do that" could be a good start.) Talk to her about how a light touch can make all the difference with someone, and how, if she can learn to show true affection in proper and positive ways, she'll be able to show friendship, compassion, and care more than most others.

Honesty and Trust

Trust is the cornerstone to most any person's character. When trust is there and honesty can be counted on, you've got a person you can depend on, even if you don't always agree with him or her. Take away trust and honesty, and a person's character is cracked at the foundation.

Why Teen Girls Lie

It will happen: your teen will lie to you. This can be heartbreaking for the parent who has said, over and over and for years and years, "as long as you are honest we can always work things out." But don't take it personally. Girls lie for many reasons, most of which are understandable, even if they are hurtful. As mentioned in Chapter 4, the first type of lying is perhaps the most innocent of all: lies to avoid disappointment. Many girls grow up wanting to please Mom and Dad (and a multitude of others). Your daughter lives on the approval she gets; she feeds off her own pride of being the "good child."

Then comes the day she slips up. Maybe she got a bad grade on a test; perhaps she did something she is not allowed to do (like wander the mall instead of go to a movie). She lies to you about it, and you find out. It is important for parents to understand that, much like a toddler, the adolescent girl may be using the lie to "wish away" the issue. (If she says it didn't happen, maybe it didn't).

 Alert

If you realize your daughter has lied, always give her the chance to tell the truth before you confront her about the lie. "Are you sure you didn't have a math test?" can help her come clean about a simple lie.

Girls may stick to their lie, hoping that you won't realize it's a lie and even, in a most childlike way, hoping the lie will come true. What's a parent to do? Once you've offered her a chance to come clean and she has not, let her know that you know the truth. Then, tell her that lying is unacceptable, and that if she had shown you the failed math test or admitted she'd roamed the mall, she might not have gotten off totally free, but she would have won your trust and respect for telling the truth. Attach to the outcome some kind of action ("For the next month, I'll walk you into the movie and out of it"). Let her know she can win back her freedom and, had she been honest, she might have won that sooner. Show her the truth pays.

The second type of lie is the testing lie. Your daughter is wondering what her boundaries are now, and as she watches other girls get away with more and more, she may wonder two things: how much can she get away with and are her parents truly watching out for her? Let's say she tells you she's going to Friday night skating when in fact she's ducking behind the building to meet up with some older boys. She may lie to see if she can get away with it; and she may also lie to see if you have her safety in mind. She might not realize she wants you to be her safety net, but she does.

 Fact

Almost all adolescent girls lie at some point. If you have never caught your daughter in a lie, you may want to look closer. While the rare child never lies, the normal child does indeed.

What should you do if you suspect your daughter is lying? It's a tough situation: you believe she's lying, but you cannot prove it until it happens. You don't want to let her sneak off to an unsafe situation, but until she does it, the lie does not really exist. Here's how one astute dad handled it:

Bernie's teen daughter was having a sleepover in their newly finished walk-out basement. That day, his younger son told him he'd overheard the daughter telling friends they'd all be sneaking out after her parents went to sleep. Rather than confront her, Bernie stayed awake and waited. When he heard the door quietly open and close, he crept outside and hopped on his bike and rode past the sneaking girls. It was 2 A.M. "Nice night for a walk!" he chirped as he pedaled past them. He never had to say another word. The girls, mortified, were back in the house in a snap. Clever indeed. Bernie was able to make the girls feel remorse, prove they had lied without ever talking about it, and kept them safe, all in one short bike ride.

When Lies Are Harmful

Girls' lies can go too far though. When your daughter is lying constantly or is lying in ways that can hurt her or others, it's time to take more direct action. Let's say your daughter has lied about her activities more than twice. You've now reached a point, sadly, where you cannot believe her when she says where she is going and what she is doing. Because her safety is your primary concern, you can no longer, for the time being, allow her to do activities that are not supervised by adults. This won't be easy on you, because, to be blunt, your daughter might just hate you for it. But remember: you are not here to be her friend. You are here to be her parent. Someday, she'll understand you were helping her and keeping her safe. Stay strong and stick to your guns. But do offer, from the start, a way for her to win back your trust and a timeline to do so. If she can see a solution, she might just eventually buy into it.

 Essential

Don't lie yourself. Even if it's something simple like, "Don't tell Mom how much we spend on this tool," a lie by you can be a subtle suggestion to your child. Honesty pays, particularly for a parent. As always, you are the role model.

What about girls who lie about each other? Your daughter may take part in this type of lying, and may have been a victim of it. Open a discussion about a time in your life when a lie about you or another girl harmed them. Don't ask your daughter to share, just tell your story. She may open up about the lies she sees hurting those around her, or she may have never realized the long-term harm lies about others can do. Either way, you're instilling and understanding in her. And remind her: if she is honest and true to her friends, she'll win their trust. And trust is the most valuable thing you can win from anyone, friend or family.

Social Responsibility

Imagine a world where all people understood they had a responsibility to take action to help the world, beyond just wearing an INSPI(RED) T-shirt? Your daughter can be part of that world, if you raise her to understand social responsibility.

Doing What Matters to You

A first step in social responsibility for a teen can be in doing what matters to her. Does she have a family member or friend who struggles with a disease or issue? That can be a nice place to begin helping the world. A fundraiser like a walk is a nice start, or calling a foundation that helps and asking where she can pitch in is a good move. Girls who are struggling can find that helping others helps themselves too. Social responsibility can offer girls the feeling of success, leadership, and good will.

If your daughter does not have a friend or family member in need, encourage her to read about different issues in the world. World hunger. Women's rights. Poverty in America. Anything that piques her interest—help her find a way to make a difference. Make sure, though, that it's a cause that truly matters to her. That buy-in could be her first step toward being a helping and positive member of society.

What Matters to the World

She may find, too, that helping in itself can be a help. Girls who volunteer for organizations generally have better self-esteem (see Chapter 6 for more on this). They also find that the rewards go far beyond just knowing they've made a difference.

First, there's the school spin: more than a few girls have found great school project subjects or essay ideas from within their volunteer work. Teachers and schools react positively to girls who work on such projects and who carry over what they have learned to the classroom.

There are other rewards as well: scholarships, award programs, and even national recognition are available to teens who volunteer. In years that can be thick with rejection and worry, such recognition can go a long way in building a girl's self-confidence and character (and scholarship money makes Mom and Dad happy too).

In the end, social responsibility may pay off but should be undertaken for its own sake and for what it is: one human reaching out and helping another human, the purest kindness that exists.

Spirituality

Each life needs a foundation, and in many families, that foundation is spirituality. Can you raise a girl who maintains hers, or who finds one she truly believes in?

Family Traditions

You are Catholic, or Jewish, or non-denominational. Your family has practiced a certain religion or spiritual tradition for years, and you want your daughter to carry that on. You've taken her to all the masses or services, given her all the lessons. What if she does not buy in? First, it's normal for teens to balk at family traditions of spirituality. It's all about their age. They're testing the waters, wondering how much of you they want to carry on and how much they want to change. Religion is a topic that runs deep for most, so having your child question it can on the surface be hurtful. And yet, it seems to happen often. The Catholic teen claims not to want confirmation, claiming she is not sure she believes in God. The Presbyterian suddenly wants to check out a Catholic Mass. What's a family to do? If possible, be flexible and help your child to look at what it is she doesn't agree with in your family religion and what you can do to address her questions. And let her know that everyone at every age often questions his or her faith. You might even want to compliment her for questioning: after all, something like Catholic confirmation is a big step that should be thought through and taken seriously.

You may want to consider being open to the idea of your child attending other religious events with friends of other denominations too. But don't leave it at that. Talk to her after about what she saw, what she liked, and how she can weave what she liked into your own chosen religion.

Non-Belief

She said it, and you're crushed: "I don't believe there is a God." Don't think you've failed. Teens question everything. Instead, see it as a chance to open up a discussion about spirituality. Perhaps you could talk about prayer and how you feel it has worked in your life. Show your child how she can use spirituality in a simple way. Point out stars or heroes (there are plenty in the sports world!) who turn to religion every day and every hour. And in the end, if your child insists, let her explore every angle. If you stick with your beliefs but respect her need to question, you may, in the end, win her back to where you hope they will be.

 Alert

Spirituality can be cool! Offer your child a leadership position in your church education program, or find a neat outdoor adventure camp run by your religion. Help her to see that religion can help her to connect with her identity and her community.

Conversely, what if you are not a believer and your child is one? Again, it is a time to allow her to explore and for you to respect her choices and challenges. But make sure she understands that she needs to respect and accept your decisions in belief issues too. And as a parent, it is your responsibility to check out any religion she may be interested in. Make sure it's a respected religion. Believe it or not, cults are still out there and teen girls can be their prey. If your child becomes interested, attend a few church meetings and learn all you can. Then, if it looks fine, respect her choice.

Chapter 10

School and Social Issues

School is your daughter's world, her social center, and the place where she experiences most of her highs and lows. While parents like to think of school as a place where children are constantly nurtured and taught, in the adolescent years, the school experience can get dicey. From the lunch table to the desk, it takes all a girl has to work through school issues.

"Mean Girls": The New "Popular"

Remember when Jan Brady ran for "most popular girl," and what it pretty much boiled down to was people just plain *liking* her? Popular has changed in recent years. Today's "popular" often means girls who control things, pick on others, and belittle "underlings." It's a daily challenge to live with or be one of those girls.

When Mean Is Cool

In any definition of *popular* in a dictionary, the words "mean" or "controlling" are unlikely to appear. So what's with today's popular? Don't be surprised to hear your daughter talking about how the "popular" girls control school. As made famous in the hit flick *Mean Girls*, popular girls today seem to hold their throne via manipulation and cruelty—both of which are forms of bullying. Is your daughter one of them? It might be hard for parents, thirsty to see their daughter in a "popular" or leadership role, to see possible "mean girl" actions and attitudes. With the iconization of "mean girls" in today's society, some parents may even secretly like their daughter wielding power, as unkind as it may be.

 Essential

> The classic book decoding this new popularity situation is *Queen Bees and Wannabes* by Rosalind Wiseman, a must-read for parents of adolescent girls.

It is important for parents not to celebrate if their daughter is the "popular" one by today's teen standards. Girls who rule with an iron tongue have their own issues and problems, and parents need to address them as well. "Popular girls" today control using intimidation. Is that the lesson you teach in your home or the way you want your daughter to act in the world as an adult? You'll need to put aside your own issues ("I was picked on as a teen; I'm so glad my daughter's not the victim like I was"), and work toward getting your daughter to understand that likeability, and not popularity, is what matters in life. As tempting as it is to work out your own horrid middle school and high school issues via your daughter, you must let her work on her own life, not yours.

Building the "All-Around Girl"

What you really want might just be a myth: a girl who is kind, friendly, compassionate, and hardworking; who cares less about her social standing in school and more about what she does to make the world a better place. Can any teen live up to that? Probably not entirely, but that does not mean parents should not work toward that goal. It is important for parents to realize that no child is perfect. Say it out loud: "All girls are mean at times." So as you look at the good in your daughter and celebrate it, you need to look also for what might be not-so-good. Is she a follower; the girl who does not do the mean act but quietly goes along with it (such as leaving another girl out of a lunch table or social plans)? Was she once the quiet girl who is now suddenly getting attention and respect from the other "popular" girls? This can be a tough situation; the girl once picked on or left out can be seduced with the glee of being on the other side.

 Alert

Try to remind your daughter of what it feels like to be left out or picked on. Can she really do that to another girl when she knows just how horrible it feels? Driving this point home can be helpful.

One key to helping a girl be a "nice girl" is helping her find a variety of activities to take part in. If she is able to play volleyball but also be in the band, she's going to interact with a cross section of the teen population and therefore learn that all different types of people can be her friends. If she can be part of a group that does community service work and be a cheerleader too, she'll see she does not have to fit into one single puzzle piece. Learning that she can mesh with all types of people is a valuable life lesson, and one that may just help her through these tough times.

Bullies and Cliques

Believe it or not, cliques can begin forming in the preschool years, and bullies can emerge from such cliques. Parents have more input and weight into the creation of these two difficult issues than they may imagine. If you participated in cliques or bullying in your youth, it's not too late to help work to change them now.

How Cliques Form

It starts at playgroup, when a bunch of parents all from the same neighborhood (and therefore the same economic background) get their children together to build friendships. It becomes more cemented when certain girls are placed on the same team or group at the tender age of six or seven and taught they are a "team," together for better or worse. Slowly, without parents realizing it, cliques begin to form. For parents, this can all happen without you even knowing. What parent does not want his or her child to go into their school years with a solid group of friends? The problem starts when girls of similar backgrounds and with similar activities get the message that those backgrounds and activities are the reason they should be friends.

 Fact

Soccer—or other sport—jackets and colors can be a visible identification of a clique. Think of it: a soccer team jacket that every girl who is on the team wears with pride at all times is not that different from gangs wearing gang colors.

Schools and teachers work to break up such groups, in some cases trying to place them in different classes and lunches, offering them a chance to mingle with, meet, and hopefully befriend girls from other walks of life. But it's not easy for schools to make happen when parents rally so strongly behind such groups and teams. That's easy to do: you like your daughter being part of a team (or program such as band or theater) particularly a winning team. But here's a novel concept: what if her sports team were not the center of her universe? And what if your friendship circle were not made up entirely of parents of those team/programs? Again, your actions, in this case reaching out to befriend many types of parents from diverse backgrounds, can send your daughter a signal that she can have friends from different backgrounds, and that cliques are not necessary for a good social life.

Bullying by Girls

The classic bully is seen as the big, tough boy who shakes down kids for their lunch money. Girls are more adept at stealth bullying. From middle school on, girl bullying, also called relational aggression, happens every day. Rather than throw a punch or shove a girl, female bullies are more likely to do something emotionally painful to another girl. Sly comments about attire. Blocking someone from sitting a particular—or any—lunch table (a vast amount of female bullying happens at school lunchtime—pay attention to what your daughter says about her lunch hour). Girls can also carry on "whisper campaigns" that bully other girls with innuendo and rumor, and they are quite good at picking on a girl for what she wears, how she talks, and even what color her hair is. This bullying is painful in a way a punch can never be, and can leave scars for a lifetime.

 Question

What if my daughter is the bully?
The best thing you can do, not only for the victims but also for her, is to seek counseling for her immediately. Many bullies derive satisfaction from inflicting suffering on others and usually defend their actions by blaming their victims in some way. This is not a healthy practice.

If your daughter is the victim of bullying, she may not share it with you. But you may suddenly see changes. If she refuses to go to school, has vague aches and pains, begins to dress in a drastically different way, changes her eating habits suddenly, or retreats socially, be on the lookout for bullying. If you suspect your daughter is being bullied, you must notify the school, even if your daughter protests. Bullying today is a crisis situation (think Columbine and the Williamsport, Pennsylvania, shootings—both incidents stemmed at least in part from bullying). Even verbal bullying needs follow up.

That's not to say girls never take part in physical bullying. Girl fights are as much a part of teen culture today as boy fights are. Schools report an increase in fights between girls each year. It is more important than ever to talk to your daughter about physical violence and condemn it. Remind her that it is a criminal offense and try to teach her how to walk away and seek help.

Smart Girls and Their Issues

Your daughter is an A+ (or close to it) student. She studies hard and is an achiever. Like all teen situations, this one comes with its own set of issues. Working closely with your high-achieving girl can help her stay that way and not go astray or go too far.

High Achievers

Some girls lean toward high achievement (and some birth order experts claim first children who are girls tend more toward this than most teens). It's a good thing: all parents want their child to excel in school. But high achievement does not come without its own problems. First, girls who tend to get high grades may not have experienced failure properly. If you've never gotten, say, a C on something, you may grow to think that anything less than straight As will ruin your life. This can lead girls to push themselves too hard and having feelings of inadequacy, even when they are excelling.

 Essential

If you have a high achiever, encourage her to try—and enjoy—an activity she may not be the best at or the star of. If she tries and cannot do it, she can learn that it's okay not to always be the best.

Girls who are high achievers can tend toward perfectionism in other ways too. Thinness is one way: some highly ambitious girls work so hard on exercise and food limiting that they can go too far. (More on eating and image issues in Chapter 14.) Their expectation of "perfection" spills over to their bodies and skews their perceptions of their own bodies. Watch your high-achieving girl closely for such issues. These girls can also become controlling in other ways. Witness Reese Witherspoon's character, Tracy Flick, in the comedy *Election*. Flick was a caricature, but not so far from what can happen to girls who are set on winning it all.

Hiding Their Abilities

During middle school years and even high school years, the smart girl who is a high achiever may suddenly feel embarrassed by her smarts. Not all girls want to be labeled as a "brainiac." They may fear the "nerd" label too, and suddenly hide from their friends their intelligence and even start to act "dumb" in some instances, still getting good grades but faking that they have no common sense around friends (particularly boys). Some girls even go as far as to stop trying in school. If you see a sudden grade slip from this type of girl, don't assume the work has gotten too hard. Talk to her about her abilities and help her find a way to embrace them. She's a lucky girl to have the gift of intelligence, and she needs to remember that.

Show her some examples of stars or athletes who are smart too. For example, Jodie Foster graduated from Yale, and Geena Davis was a "mathlete." If you can encourage her to see that well-rounded people are those who know to use and celebrate their intelligence (and not flaunt it), she may just not mind being the "brainiac."

Girls with Educational Challenges

If your daughter has faced educational challenges all these years, from learning disabilities to just plain struggling to do average work, it probably didn't make a huge difference in early years. But come the adolescent years, girls with these issues can struggle with their public image, and might even feel shame.

Class Levels

In grade school, most girls with educational challenges were streamlined into "regular" classes, given modified learning plans, and sometimes pulled out of class for short periods for extra attention. But come middle school and high school, most schools begin leveling subjects. For instance, a high school freshman English class may be offered in three ways: accelerated, college sequence, and basic skills. If your daughter has struggled with learning disabilities, there is a chance she might land in that "basic skills" level. Unfortunately, mean kids and even most students are biased against that level, thinking of students in there as the "short bus kids" or "sped kids." SPED, standing for special education, is a hot-button label for most girls, and a hurtful one, although it should not be.

 Alert

Don't push your daughter into a higher level for just social reasons. But do talk to her guidance counselor. With extra tutoring at home, you may be able to move her up a level if she wishes.

Girls in lower class levels may rebel, acting as though school does not matter to them anymore. If you see signs of this, you and her guidance counselor need to drive home the fact that no matter what level she is placed in at school, she's working toward the same goal as all students in the school: college and/or a career that supports her financially and fulfills her as a person. It might be a good idea to find a celebrity, successful adult, or friend you have whom she admires who struggled with learning issues as a child. Show her that success will be hers just as much as it will be for a girl in accelerated classes, so long as she does her best and tries hardest.

Excelling in Other Places

Many parents of girls who struggle educationally try to find other areas for them to excel at school. Sports and clubs are a good option. If your daughter can star as a field hockey player even as she struggles in class, she may feel more comfortable in the school community. She will also make friends with girls she might not come across in her classes. The same goes for civic groups such as student council and volunteer groups that help the world. Encourage your daughter to find places besides the classroom to shine in at her school. The successes there may help fuel a drive to do the best she can in her classes. But don't let her other activities be the sole focus of her school days. She is there to learn, and classes and schoolwork do matter.

The Importance of Getting Involved

Well-rounded girls (and adults as well) have a variety of activities in their lives. They don't just go to school or work; they take part in sports or clubs or hobbies. Getting your daughter started in such activities at this age is a good way to steer a girl toward a well-rounded adult life.

Social Responsibility Clubs

The push by colleges for kids to have community service experience and the push by many high schools to require community service hours for graduation is a good thing for our girls and can help them learn that the world does not rotate around them, that there are issues more difficult than those they face every day, and that they have the power to help others. Many schools have clubs that mentor foster children, raise money for world hunger, battle drunk driving, or help the elderly. Ask your daughter to bring home a list of clubs her school has and go over it with her. Talk to her about what moves and motivates her, and then help her find a place to help the world.

 Fact

A study done by Lifetime Television found that volunteer work ranks as the most important aspect of their lives for women in their twenties. Women looking back on high school and college years saw it as the greatest influence on their adult selves.

Be sure to encourage your daughter to stick with what she chooses and not slack off on her duties. Clubs can sometimes be a lot of work, but she can learn from the work in a way that can help her grow as a person and—bonus!—help her in school. Many an essay for English class has come from such experiences, and other projects have as well. And on a day when she might feel like everything went wrong (a fight with a good friend; boy troubles; a so-so grade on a test), she can always look at what she has done to help the world and know, even on the worst days, she's making a difference.

Tangible Rewards

Another bonus to social activism is this: there are many awards out there for kids who do for the world to win. Even if your daughter is not one who will ever win an academic scholarship, she might just be a star in the social activism world. Two of the most prestigious awards given to students who help the world are the Prudential Spirit of Community Award and the Do Something Award. Encourage your daughter to Google these awards and read about the other kids who have been honored. She might just be one of them someday.

Girl and Social Aspects of Sports

There is no doubt that participating in sports helps a girl in many ways. From physical fitness to learning how to be a team player, sports help girls in many ways. But like all things with adolescent girls, there are challenges.

Team Good versus Team Bad

It's good to be part of a team. A girl learns to do what is best for the group instead of just for herself, and learns to be friends with (or at least to respect) girls from other backgrounds. Team sports also teach girls how to respect and do what a leader (the coach) asks them to, and how to be gracious about losing or letting someone other than her help the team win for the team's sake. All this is good. But as mentioned earlier, team sports in the adolescent years can breed some issues. Teams, particularly teams that win a lot, can become a clique of sorts. Parents play a role in this: they are so proud of their daughter's team, they may identify with it themselves.

For "club" teams (that is, non-school teams), girls may have late night practices and weekend long events. You may want to consider, as she moves toward high school, if this is really the best idea. High school takes up a lot of time and energy, and if she's part of school teams, that may be enough. Some school coaches encourage girls to form "club teams" off-season as a way to practice as a whole and get around school athletic rules (most school systems nationally do not allow teams to practice as such in the off-season). If you feel it is too much and yet think that your daughter might be "punished" by the coach for not participating, quietly speak to your school's athletic director about the situation. Teams that are caught doing this risk having their entire school's athletic program suspended, sometimes for a full year.

 Essential

Try not to let a team sport rule your daughter and your family's life. Yes, it is fun to watch and cheer for them, but don't talk about it all the time and don't steer her toward making the team her entire life.

Surviving the Cut

While most youth sports do not allow cuts and most schools try to have freshman sports programs that allow kids to play no matter what their ability at least that one year, there is going to come a time your daughter faces a possible cut. How can a parent handle it? If your daughter plays soccer and is average at best (but loves it all the while), and her high school soccer program is highly competitive, it may be time to sit down with her and talk about why she plays a team sport. True, she has been tied to this sport and this group of girls for what seems like forever, but could she consider trying another sport just for the sake of exercise, team spirit, and fun?

 Alert

> Come high school, parents have no say in cuts. Most schools have a strict rule that parents cannot talk to coaches about cuts or playing time, no matter how unfair they feel the coach's decision is. It is now up to your daughter to have that talk with the coach.

A cut can rock a girl to her core. She'll fear rejection from her group of friends who made the team, and question her ability in everything. If she does get cut, be ready for some tears and some rough moments. It will be your job to help her see that there are other ways to be involved and feel like a part of her school. As for the friends, find ways to get them all together even if she isn't on the team. And there is always the manager option: every team needs a student manager. If she really wants to stay a part of that group, encourage her to talk to the coach about how and if she can in ways other than playing. And if she does not, show her this is a time to seek out new things to do with her free time, be it a sport, and art or a hobby. And remember, if your daughter is the one who makes the team and another girl is cut, teach her to keep that girl in her social sphere and to help that girl see the sport was not everything.

If your daughter has her heart set on making a team but you suspect she may not, get her ready. Tell her about a time you got cut and what you did instead (hopefully you found something new to do with your time you loved just as much). And give her examples of star athletes who struggled as a kid. Does she know superstar Tom Brady of the New England Patriots spent most of his high school games on the bench? All is not lost. She has years to live and play sports ahead of her.

 Question

Does body type play into who gets cut at sports?
Yes, to a point. A girl who was once a great swimmer never grows tall. Or a girl who was a star gymnast grows bigger. It's important not to marry your daughter to one sport before she has developed, because everything can change as her body does.

"Cool" Sports

Every school has its cool sports and its not-so-cool sports, at least in the eyes of the students (and sometimes the faculty and parents). What if your daughter is part of a sport that does not get as much attention, such as gymnastics or tennis? Work as a parent to make it change. Call the local newspaper and offer to help them post results each week. Ask the principal to come to a match or meet or two. Go there and cheer them on yourself. And remind your daughter, it's not about being on a "cool" sport; it's about being on a sport that works for her both emotionally and physically. In the end, if you can find a sport that fulfills your daughter's physical and social needs—even if she's never considered it before—that will be a championship effort.

Chapter 11

Let's Talk about Sex (and Dating)

It starts earlier and earlier in the lives of girls today. The pressure to date, to be in a relationship, and yes, to get physical comes sooner than most parents can imagine or want to envision. By talking through the pressures she faces and being open about what's going on out there, parents can help a girl navigate this new world, or at the very least, know some of what is going on in her life outside your home.

Handling "The Talks"

"The Talk" isn't easy to initiate or to keep going, but it's your job as the parent of a twenty-first-century girl to make sure it does. So be prepared, one might say, and learn how to help her be open or at least educated.

It Has to Happen

She's not going to want to do it, and chances are you'll be leery about it too. Talking about sex and boys is uncomfortable at best, but simply needs to be done. Even if your mother still has yet to have "that talk" with you, don't repeat history. Your openness will open your daughter's mind to sharing her concerns, fears, and perhaps even experiences with you. Keep in mind there are two kinds of girls: those who would rather die than talk about this, and those who seem more open than you can imagine. Okay, there are a million other types in between that. No matter which your girl is, you need to make "The Talk" happen—for her good and for your own.

 Fact

According to the AWARE Foundation, a group that studies sex and teens, children whose parents talk to them about sex are more likely to talk about it themselves and to delay their first sexual experience.

When to Start the Conversation

Most public schools in America start true sex education at about fifth grade. Smart parents stay ahead of the school and start their own talks, using the school programs as additional information and support. This means you may need to begin your talks with your daughter before the onset of puberty is evident. And while your daughter may never realize it, this may just be as frightening and uncomfortable for you as it is for her.

Parents can get booklets from their health care providers to help them with the talk—and in many cases, the health care provider will also initiate the discussion.

So when to have "The Talk"? Puberty is starting earlier and earlier for girls, and could begin when your daughter is as young as nine years of age. By that time, you will want to have begun to talk about the basics, or even earlier, if, say, a five-year-old child asks where babies come from; avoid the whole "stork" routine. Rather, use simple words without a lot of detail to tell your child the truth. That will lay the groundwork for future dialogue. Keep in mind, the earlier you've made such conversations "normal," the easier they will come in the more critical years. But what if you've not made them normal and your daughter is just reaching middle school? It's never too late to open the window of communication.

 Essential

A good way to start a conversation you might not be comfortable with is by sharing a magazine article on sexuality with your daughter. Ask her to read it and then ask her what she thinks about it. By starting a discussion about information presented in a relatively objective, impersonal way, you'll both feel more at ease.

When your daughter is older, there is more of a chance that she will balk at such conversations. She's embarrassed, she thinks she knows everything already, and the *last* thing she wants to do is even imagine that her parent knows anything about sex, much less participates in it. It's up to you to be the adult and to make the conversation appropriate, and most importantly, to make it happen. This means finding a place that is as comfortable as the time. At a busy restaurant in the presence of her brother is obviously not the answer; nor is a quick chat in the middle of breakfast before she's heading to school.

Instead, set aside some time alone, be it at home or somewhere else, where the two of you both feel comfortable and when you have the time to dive into the issues with her. Timing is everything; but so is location. Some parents find bedtime is a good time for such talks. The dark makes the child less nervous and the comfort helps both parents and child relax into and intimate conversation. The car or during a good walk are also a good places because she doesn't have to look at you face to face, which makes it easier to talk about tough or embarrassing topics.

What to Say

Needless to say, shock factor is not a good thing here. You'll want to start out with simple concepts: gauge what she wants to know and then add some to it (because she surely needs to know more than she wants to). Let's say your preteen is curious about unmarried sexual relations. You'll want to talk to her about the urges that come with sex, and what she might feel. You need to let her know (particularly in the case of girls who develop early) that just because she feels those urges does not mean she is in any way ready for them or has to give into them. Explain abstinence, and also the remorse that many girls can feel years later from a poor sexual decision as a young girl. Additionally you should talk to your daughter about sexual responsibility, contraception, and prevention of sexually transmitted diseases (STDs).

 *Question*

What if she asks about my sexual history?
It is not necessary to share your own sexual history. However, some girls do benefit from hearing their own mother's happiness or disappointment about a sexual decision she made as a young girl.

You may also want to use pop culture figures as springboards to conversations. Your daughter has been besieged by the media with information she may not fully understand. When you say what you say, it is vital that you always be honest—even if it means saying "I don't know about that, but we can look it up together or I can look it up for you." Most parents will want to tell a girl not to take part in sex at this point in her life. But today, you'll need to explain to her what "not taking part in sex" really means. In the end, you'll want her to not only understand the physical ramifications of sexual activity (such as STDs and pregnancy), but also the emotional ramifications as well. Talk about how being in a sexual relationship can toy with the minds of even smart adult women: how is a growing girl supposed to deal with that? Talk about "pride in ownership." It's her body to cherish, save, and respect.

Doing something to take that away might just have repercussions that stay with her for a lifetime.

Masturbation

With boys, it's a must-have talk. Masturbation is expected. But for girls, it's long been hush-hush. Even today, the thought is "good girls don't, but good boys do." The reality is, girls, like boys, are curious about their bodies and may experiment with self-pleasing. Talking about it can be the biggest challenge a parent faces, because girls and masturbation have long been a silent issue.

What to Expect

Think of it this way: ever since magazines like *Cosmopolitan* started printing stories on how to "find your G-spot," more and more females have been more open about masturbation. Studies show that 80 percent of males have masturbated by the age of eighteen, and that's no surprise. But they also show that 60 percent of girls have as well. So it's best you assume your daughter might be one of them. Usually around the time of puberty, girls start wondering about such things and even talking about it. Your daughter may stumble upon the idea in conversation or, in this day and age, on the Web. It's a good idea to have a talk with her at this time about what masturbation is. Try, as difficult as it is, to be frank and honest.

It's best to keep in mind that this is all probably new to her too. She may experience her first orgasm on her own, and may need you to explain that many women do so as way to know, in the future, how to help a man (or a woman if she is gay) help her reach that point. But also let her know that she is too young for sex, even if she can get her body to react that way. Talk about abstinence and encourage her to consider it, even when it comes to masturbation. Make sure she understands: just as sex is perfectly acceptable among consenting adults, masturbation is acceptable for women. It might just be a bit early now.

 Alert

If you "catch" your daughter masturbating, don't freak out. Rather, ask her to gather herself together and then have a talk with you. Let her know it is not a punishable thing.

Setting Rules

You will need to explain the rules of masturbation. It's never to be done in public. It's never to be done in the presence of another girl or boy (because really, that does constitute a sexual act and as a parent, you feel she is too young for that quite yet). If she finds she feels the need to do it frequently, encourage her to talk to you about it. Sexual addiction can start early, and you'll want to help her learn to control her desires and needs in an acceptable way.

Dating 101

Going out. Hooking up (and remember: hooking means intercourse in many circles today). Going steady. It's all out there for girls, as early as the fourth grade. Parents can help their daughter understand this world and find a way to not celebrate it but rather keep it in check.

Age and Dating

You thought it was cute when your first-grader talked about her "boyfriend," but suddenly in fifth grade, it all seems to be getting a bit too real for you. "Dating" is beginning earlier and earlier in life for kids today, in part might be thanks to Hollywood: how many movies has your girl seen where the young heroine falls in love? Part of it also has to do with society as a whole. More and more things seem to come earlier in life. Middle school semi-formals are an example. So what age is the right age to date? The answer is not as simple as "sixteen years old," and is different for each child. It comes down to you as a parent and your child as an informed partner deciding that she is mature enough, responsible enough, and strong enough to begin to date.

 Alert

Be wary of peer and parent-peer pressure around this debate. Don't let the parent living her past dating life vicariously through her daughter affect you and your daughter's decision on this issue.

You may first want to ask your daughter what exactly "going out" means to her. If it means—as it does in many young girls cases—immediately ignoring the boy she is "going out" with and doing nothing more than write his name over and over on her instant message profile, you may feel that is fine. You may also want to make sure she's not putting herself in a social situation she is not ready for. Is it expected, in her social circle, that anyone "going out" kisses? Let her know that she can—and should—make her own decisions on such topics. If "going out" means actually dating, you'll want to assess your daughters emotional maturity and decide if she is ready. Like it or not, boys pressure girls (and girls pressure boys) to do things and get into sexual situations they might not be ready for. Your preteen older daughter may not be ready, and your not allowing her to date at all may be the safety net she needs. Even when she is thirteen, her cognitive development isn't capable of handling these situations. It cannot hurt to say no for a while. In the end, it will be up to you. Even if she chooses to "go out" with someone, if you forbid her to be alone with a boy, there will be no "real" dating.

Types of Dates

Girls usually ease their way into dating via group dates— usually to the movies or the mall or the mini-golf links in your town. You'll notice when it begins. Don't think that this group setting ensures nothing inappropriate can happen. If you or your daughter are not ready for dating and personal relationships, she should only be allowed to do such things with adult supervision, even in a group setting. But if you are just about ready, a group date can be a good first step. Your daughter won't feel awkward and will be surrounded by friends should she decide she's in too deep. Talk to your daughter about a coed event that is planned. Who will be there? What exactly will they be doing? Does she have any worries or fears?

Fact

Spin the Bottle and other such games still exist. If you have a coed group hanging out in your family room, make regular trips through the room. Let them know that they're never really alone, and such games will not begin.

Then there is the time it happens: your daughter asks to go out alone on what can only be construed (no matter what she calls it) as a "real date." Don't lock the doors and seal the windows and threaten her. Instead, take a deep breath and, with her help, decide if it's something she is ready for. First, is the boy any older than her? This is not always the biggest issue; plenty of girls mature more rapidly than boys. But a boy who has a driver's license and whose friends are having sex with older girls might be a situation your younger daughter is not ready for. Talk to her about it, and if you feel ready to say yes, do so with confidence and support. Your daughter is probably as nervous, if not more nervous, than you are about it. Don't worry about being old-fashioned: no boy should ever beep his horn in your driveway to summon your daughter. A ring of the doorbell and a brief hello should be expected before they depart. But don't go too far the other way either. "What are your intentions with my daughter" truly is a caricature and at this point, should stay that way.

Don't dismiss your own hunches too. Moms tend to have great "radar." If you feel a bad situation in the works, end it before it starts. And always give her another way to get home if needed in a crunch: money for a cab or a sibling's cell phone. The message is: if you need to leave a situation, do it in a safe and quick way, and Mom can help you any way you need.

 Essential

Devise code words with your daughter that she can use to alert you to help her get out of an uncomfortable situation. If she calls you and says the code word, that means you should demand she come home immediately. She'll be safe and can "blame" her departure on you.

Polite Dating

You'll want to talk to your daughter about dating etiquette too. While she should never ditch a boy, neither should she ever stay in a situation she is uncomfortable in. Give her a "free pass," a note or a coin that she can "trade in" for you to help get her out of *any* situation that goes too far. That would mean you'd have to help her get out of the situation and get home without any punishment. Let her know that by using it, she'll be saving the punishment, saving herself, but also clue-ing you into things that you might otherwise not already know about. In other words, you'll help her be safe and not punish her; but that does not mean you won't think more carefully about what you allow her to do in the future. Chances are, if she ends up needing the "pass," she'll need you to give her more boundaries anyway.

Alert

Train your daughter *never* to leave a drink unattended. That way no one can ever slip anything into it when she is not looking. Overprotective? There's no such thing. Demand she keep this rule for herself.

Date Rape

It's real, and it happens. You'll need to talk to your daughter before she ever starts dating about the basics of date rape. Help her to understand that no always means no, and that if she is not listened to, she needs to scream or seek help immediately. Also let her know that if date rape happens, she is a victim and should not feel ashamed or afraid. Particularly in the case of an immature or inexperienced girl, date rape can be confusing. Did I cause it myself? Did I ask for it? By letting her know ahead of any chance of this happening that those questions will run through her head, you'll help her recognize them. The best defense, though, is keeping her out of situations in which it could happen. Don't know a boy well or have never seen his car around town? Just put your foot down and say no to the date. Heard a boy is bad news but see your girl drawn to him? Make sure she only sees him in groups or does not see him at all. In the end, the best thing she can know is that you are there for her to help her in any situation ever, and that should she be abused during a date, she deserves to be defended and the boy deserves to be punished.

You'll want to teach your daughter and keep your eye out for any signs of dating violence too. It happens, even to strong, dependable girls. Don't think the signs are just bruises and breaks. With teens (and sadly this is common) signs include a date who keeps a girl away from family and friends, cutting her off from any support she may be able to get (sadly, teen girls can see this as "love," as in "he only wants me to be with him"). Verbal abuse and/or extreme jealousy is a sign too. Alert your daughter to the signs, and watch for them yourself. If you have a strong feeling, immediate intervention is required.

Coping with Breakups

That first time your little girl's heart is broken you are going to want to spit nails. But you need to practice control. Yes, show her that you care. But also let her know she's young and most likely will experience all sorts of relationships and meet all kinds of boys in the future. Share with her photos and stories of your old flames (without giving too many details). Let her see that most people experience heartbreak and survive it.

And then there are your feelings. It's hard for a parent not to despise a boy when he hurts their daughter, but it's in your best interest to keep your feelings to yourself. Remember when you were in high school and your best friend broke up with her boyfriend? You finally told her how much you hated him. Five years later, that was one wedding you were not invited to. Love can be crazy, and even if it is your child, you should temper your opinions just in case. In the end, the one she loves is her choice, not yours.

Alert

If a girl lingers too long in her grief over a lost love—or does something to harm herself after a breakup, you may want to have her talk to a professional about it. Clinical depression can come in many ways, and you don't want to downplay it.

Sexual Pressure and Where It Comes From

Girls today feel all sorts of pressure: pressure to be popular, to fit in, and to be "loved" by the masses. That can translate to pressure to do things you might never dream they would attempt to do.

Pressure from Boys

"If we don't do it we get sick." Or, "You'd do it if you loved me." Or better yet, "It's not sex if there is no penetration." These lines have been mysteriously handed down through the ages from one adolescent boy to the next. And somehow, with the twinkling of the stars or the crashing of the beach waves luring them on, girls fall for it. Getting a girl to understand what pressure feels like and why she should listen to her gut is a good exercise leading up to the dating years. Let her know that boys will say such things, and that she might even almost believe them. But if something feels a tiny bit not right, she's better off erring on the side of caution. Put it to her this way: If she says "not now" but "maybe later," there will always be a chance to do what it is she thinks she wants to do after getting home and assessing the situation. If she says "okay" when she's not 100 percent sure, she can never go back and erase that act. And what if your daughter is the one pressuring the boy? Try to instill in her that just as she would not want to be pushed, neither should she push a boy.

Pressure from Friends

"Oh come on, he's hot! Just do it already!" Or, "You're the only one in our grade who hasn't done it yet! Virgin loser!" Or better yet, "It's not sex if there is no penetration." Girls can pressure one another to engage in sex as much as boys can. Try to let your daughter know first off that what she's hearing just might not be true, and the very girl pressuring her might never have had sex herself. Also try to instill in her a self-worth that rises above having to do what the crowd (claims it) does. It might surprise your daughter to find out that other girls would lie to her to force her into a sexual situation with a boy. Let her know that adults don't discuss what they do and with whom (at least, most don't) and that when the time comes that she engages in a sexual relationship, it won't be for the benefit of her friends. It also could come back and slap her in the face. More than once girls have egged another girl on to performing a sexual act with a boy, only to label her "slut" in front of the whole school after the fact. Hearing that warning from you might help your daughter to avoid such a situation.

Types of Sex Today

Sure it's all still done the same way Adam and Eve or who- ever started all this did it, but kids today (and some adults) have some unique views on what is sex and what is not. You'll need to know what you are talking about before talking to your kids.

"Friends with Benefits"

"Friends with benefits" ("FWBs") seem to have surfaced in the late 1990s or early 2000s. "FWBs" are friends who do not date and do not plan to date but who have sexual relations. Boys like to call girls who will give them oral sex with no real obligation their "FWBs," and some girls take pride in having them too. You need to explain to your daughter that truly, there is no such thing as unconnected sex, and that her body and her self are precious commodities that she should not just dole out to anyone at all. Talk to her about the reason adults have sex in relationships. It is okay to be honest about the physical high sex gives you, but explain that with it comes an emotional connection that is an important part of the act. She should only want to feel sex that way.

 Fact

According to a poll by the National Campaign to Prevent Teen Pregnancy, two-thirds of teen girls who had sexual relations wish they had not.

If for some reason you hear that being a "FWB" is "cool" in your daughter's school or circle, discuss it with her immediately. Talk to her about her pride and self-worth, and encourage her not to share her body with *anyone* except someone she is truly, in a grown-up way, in love with. Of course she'll feel like she's in love, and that's an issue too, but to have sex with a friend who she never plans to have a relationship with? Explain how she'll feel about it looking back twenty-five years from now.

Technical Virginity

Some girls today believe that so long as they never have penetration, they are still virgins. According to this line of thought, oral sex, anal sex, and dry-humping mean they are still virgins. You need to let your daughter know that sex is sex, and whether or not her vagina has been penetrated won't matter to her self-esteem or to her reputation. In the end, close, personal and intimate contact of any kind is going to affect her and affect her relationships. Encourage her to view them all in the same way.

How to Handle It If She Does

So you've tried it all: honest talks, lots of lessons, and still she decides to have sex. What's a parent to do? Stay calm and keep her safe.

The Initial Reaction

You'll want to cry, and it's okay if you do. After all, your little girl will never be a "little girl" again in some ways. But don't be hysterical. If she tells you herself, you need to take a deep breath and praise her for her honesty. Then talk to her about the situation. How did the decision come to be? Would she change any of it if she could? If you sense she is in over her head, help her get out of the situation. Let her blame it on you, and tell the boy she is not allowed to see him anymore. If she feels she cannot change things but wants to, get her some counseling so that she can learn to stand up for what she wants and know that she does not have to have sex if she does not want to.

 Alert

Any girl who is having sexual relations, regardless of age, needs to have a gynecological exam (pelvic) immediately. If her health care provider does not perform this service, bring your daughter to someone who does, preferably a gynecologist or woman's health practitioner with experience in performing these exams on teenagers.

You might want to scream too, but this is not a good idea. If you are upset, particularly if you find out on your own (often parents find condoms in a girl's room or worse, hear from another parent), calm yourself down and find a way to bring it up like the mature parent you are. If she lies to you, offer for her to see a gynecologist on her own, without you knowing details (Mom can't get the details anyhow because of confidentiality issues, and knowing that may convince more girls to go). Better that she practice safe sex than that she hide it from you and make mistakes. You'll want to let her know that she needs to be open with you. If she believes in what she is doing and whom she is doing it with, there should be a time she can talk calmly and openly to her loving parent about it. Give her the support she needs and let her know that you'll be ready the moment she's ready. But what if she's too young? This, again, is a case of you giving her the opportunity. It's easy enough to keep tabs on a thirteen- or fourteen-year-old girl if you put your mind to it. Remember, as her parent, you are indeed her protector. And that is not always easy.

The Long-Term Plan

If she ends up at, say sixteen, in a relationship that she insists is going to be physical, you'll want to make sure she has the right protection and she understands the risks. It's not just about pregnancy (which is a real risk—be sure to share with her stats on how many women get pregnant using birth control). You'll also want to share with her the long-term impact of birth control. If she's on the pill, she needs to know that smoking is absolutely not an option, because the combination can be life threatening. She needs to understand the many STDs that she can come across, and that one person could be having sex with others. It's the old adage: you're not just sleeping with him; you're sleeping with everyone he ever slept with. Girls seem to think that they are too smart to let such things happen. Remind her that women with degrees from Harvard have contracted STDs. No one is smarter than a virus. In the end, it will be up to you to be supportive yet educational, and to always let her know you'll help her do what is best for her long-term, and what will serve her best for a lifetime.

Sexual Orientation

Gay or straight? How about bisexual? While some gay and bisexual adults claim to have known since birth what their orientation is, the teen years are rough ones for them; years they may fight who they really are or may be confused. The good parent knows how to help a daughter look at how she feels and sort out who she is. Hard work indeed—even psychological experts have yet to delve deeply into this issue.

 Alert

It's no surprise that girls (and all teens) are mean. If your daughter wants to keep her sexual orientation private, that is fine; there is no need to make her sexual orientation public at this age. She's too young for sex anyway.

If She Thinks She is Gay

Your daughter may find herself attracted to another girl. Does this mean she is gay? The question will swirl in her mind. By educating her before this might happen, you may help her come to the answer easier.

First, it is important for girls to know that in the teen years, they may feel attraction to someone from the same sex and not be gay. Most doctors agree that homosexuality arises partly from genetics and partly from the environment a person grows up in. They also agree that girls can have an attraction to another girl and not be gay. You'll want to tell your daughter that the rules are the same regardless of whether she is attracted to boys or girls: she is not to act out her sexual desires at this young age. However, if she feels that she is always attracted to girls and never to boys, she should talk to you.

If she suspects she is gay, she may fight that feeling. After all, even in today's more open society, being gay is not an easy road. And teens who don't want to feel different in the first place may be initially horrified at the idea. Send her the message from an early age that being gay does not make someone any less a good person. Show your daughter, through your actions, how you accept people regardless of their sexual orientation.

 Essential

She can also talk to a professional if you feel it is needed. Better that she talk this through with someone (even if it is not you) than with no one.

If She Is Gay

So she comes to the point where she knows it: she's gay. This can be a difficult time for a child and a parent. First, even after you embrace her with all your love for the person she is, you may feel heartbreak and worry. Will she be discriminated against? How will she have a family? How will you work at making all your lives "normal?" You, parent, will need to tackle these personal issues without projecting them onto your daughter. This way, you'll be the first person she sees that she truly does not need to feel shame.

When and if her sexual orientation does become public, she could face some public ridicule. It takes a strong girl (and a strong woman) to "come out" as a lesbian. Chances are, your gay daughter will do this with you, her family, first, and then with a few close friends. As she builds confidence and supporters, she'll be ready to come out to the world. But don't make it on your terms; let it be on hers, She'll know when the time is right. If she wants to be public and vigilant about it, you'll need to be ready to support her and possibly take some heat of your own. Remember, parents are often "blamed" for homosexual children by those who rally against homosexuality.

 Fact

Teens who don't deal well with rejection around this topic are at higher risk for depression, dropping out of school, and substance abuse. Give her all your support and get her help.

It is important to remember that the same rules you'd have for a heterosexual daughter will be in place for a homosexual daughter. She's too young for sex. She needs to practice safe sex if she does do it. And she needs to work slowly toward mature relationships, not dive headfirst into one she is too immature to handle. If you can get past the struggles and treat the situation just as you would if your daughter were heterosexual, both you and your daughter will be better able to deal with it.

Chapter 12

Risky Business

It would be nice to think that the worst trouble your daughter will ever get into could be filed under "shenanigans," but the smart parent knows never to assume trouble is not possible. By learning all you can about potential risky behavior, knowing how to talk to your daughter about it without sounding insane, and knowing how to spot clues without overreacting, you may, in the end, get your wish.

Handling "The Other Talks"

Like talks on sex, the *last* thing your daughter wants is to talk to you about drinking, drugs, and other behaviors. Why? First, she thinks you know nothing and second, she thinks you know nothing.

Getting Clued In

Remember when all you had to do was flip on the afterschool special to find out what teen issues were and how families were dealing with them? (Don't laugh. *Sixteen and*

Pregnant, featuring Kirsten Dunst in her first after-school special, is probably still playing in your daughter's health class.) Today's parents have to do a lot more research to be clued in enough to know what they need to for frank discussions and, if needed, timely intervention. No matter whether the topic is sex, drug use, cigarettes, or new, "twenty-first century issues" like inhalants, the choking game, and more, you'll want to make sure, first and foremost, that you know what you are talking about.

 Essential

Ask your child's school for the health curriculum and learn it yourself, a step ahead of when your child does. You may learn something new or rethink something you never considered, and you'll know what your child is hearing at school.

The Internet is a good way to get clued in too, but be wary of what you read. Be sure the source is reliable. (For help deciding if a site is reliable, go to *www.fda.gov/oc/opacom/evalhealthinfo.html*) Don't let unreliable sources alarm you or worse, lead you to misdirect your child. And what about learning from other parents what dangers are out there for your child? Don't discount them, but don't take their word as gospel either. Let's say another parent tells you a lot of children in your daughter's grade have been smoking cigarettes (or drinking). Rather than approach your daughter with a "Mrs. Jones says," read up on the statistics of how many kids her age smoke, and then try to poll some parents of older kids: have they noticed such behavior as kids grow up? Then decide if it's something you need to discuss in more detail with your child.

Talking Never Hurts

Keep in mind that talking about a potential risky situation is never going to hurt anything, so it's always better to bring it up then shy away from it. The notion that parents can introduce a potential risky behavior to a child is not a reality. Wishing away a potential issue or hoping that by never addressing it you'll never have to deal with it is as dangerous as the "wishful thinking" your child may do around lies and risky behavior. Set the example by finding somewhat less awkward and always mature ways to talk about risky behaviors with your child. In the end, you'll be glad you were open from the start, even if it was uncomfortable for both of you from time to time.

Smoking

With all that is known about the dangers of smoking today, one would think the industry would be dead. And yet, teens still choose to smoke. Don't think trying it is a given. Rather, work to educate your child all you can to make the "right choice."

Peer Pressure and Smoking

Your child may grow up thinking smoking is *not* cool, and make a big display out of it when she is younger. But something shifts as girls become teens (and it is important to note here that girls have now surpassed boys in cigarette use). First, just about every fashion model on earth is a smoker (and this instills in girls' still impressive minds that smoking equates to thinness, just one of the many issues around the choice to smoke or not). Somehow, certain teen girls decide that anything they thought was uncool as a kid *must* be cool now that they are "mature" teens. They may feel peer pressure from their friends who decide to try smoking, and that's a powerful force to fight.

 Fact

In the 1990s, the American Cancer Society launched a nation-wide program called the "Smoke-Free Class of 2000," with the goal of having that class graduate from high school smoke-free. Despite millions of dollars poured into it, it failed.

Don't assume because your child is a "jock" or a "brain" that she will not smoke either. Remember, all kids of all types face pressure and also mirror what they see in pop culture from time to time. More than a few Hollywood teen celebrities have been shown with cigarettes dangling from their mouths in magazines and on TV. No girl is completely immune from that. So what do you do? Try to educate your child from the start and all the way through the realities of smoking. Do not depend on the cigarette company Web sites, as willing as they now seem to be to share information on kids and smoking and the dangers. Instead, make clear your rules and keep them known. Children do not smoke in your family, period. Let your daughter know your own personal ramifications ("If I find that you have smoked I'll lose trust in you and not be able to give you some freedoms" is a good one). Remind her and stick to it.

When Mom or Dad Is a Smoker

Is it hypocritical not to allow your child to smoke if you smoke? Not at all. It is illegal to purchase cigarettes as a minor or for a minor. As an adult, it *is* legal for you to smoke. That's the clear difference. But what about the ethics of smoking? Sure, it's your right, but as your daughter grows, this might be a good time to set an example and attempt to quit. As you try, let her share the experience with you so she can see how powerful and addictive an agent tobacco is. Help her see the danger. Explain how much you want to not smoke and what you'd give to turn time back and have never started. Even if you fail over and over, you might win her respect and at the very least, teach her a valuable lesson in battling addiction. Or better yet, she can experience teaching you a lesson. Cigarette smoking is the single most preventable cause of premature death in the United States. Each year, more than 400,000 Americans die from cigarette smoking. In fact, one in every five deaths in the United States is smoking related. Every year, smoking kills more than 276,000 men and 142,000 women.

Show her respect too by not smoking where it is not allowed or where it endangers the health of others. Don't smoke in your car even when she's not with you. Don't smoke in the house ever, and don't smoke around others. Show her that you understand the danger secondhand smoke can present to others and that while you are battling your own addiction, you will not let it hurt her or anyone else. If you can at least do that, she'll believe you when you talk of the other dangers of smoking too and hopefully, take heed.

 Alert

It is okay to tell your daughter that addiction is often familial. If you ended up addicted to smoking, chances are if she starts, she will too. And while smoking does not lead directly to other addictions, those who become addicted to smoking tend to become addicted to other vices they try.

Alcohol

Today's teens, despite a nationwide drinking age of twenty-one, are no less likely to drink than were the generations before them. Alcohol is still available and the pressure to partake hits almost every girl.

Peer Pressure and Alcohol

Girls and drinking. Think Drew Barrymore as a preteen (and then as a teen in rehab). One would think that would have been a valuable lesson to Hollywood girls and all girls. Now think Lindsay Lohan, the Olsen twins, and others. They all frequent bars and are pictured drinking from a young age. And this seems to be celebrated by teen girls, who pressure each other. They believe that if they are grown-up and cool (which they are sure they are), they should be drinking too. Here, you'll want to first message to your daughter a simple fact: underage drinking is illegal and not allowed in your family. Make sure it is clear that this rule goes with her everywhere she goes, even at a friend's house where drinking is allowed. Because ironically, some of the "peer pressure" on your daughter here may come from *your* peers. Somewhere along the line, parents became misguided, and began thinking if their daughters just drank at home or with supervision, that would be fine. This is not the case. Studies show the younger a girl starts drinking, the more chance she has of becoming addicted to alcohol. And again, it's illegal. Period.

 Fact

According to the American Medical Association, the average age at which a girl first tries alcohol is now down to thirteen years old. And according to studies, alcohol *does* affect girls differently; because they have less body water, it hits them more quickly.

There seems to be a feeling out there, too, that certain teen events simply must involve alcohol. The prom, for one. Homecoming is another. Some parents like to host "stay-at-the-house" parties and allow this to happen, thinking they are controlling things. They are not. Such activity is illegal and you, as a parent, need to just say "no" on behalf of your daughter. She may hate you for it at the time, and may utter those all-too-often-heard words "but I'm the only girl in town who can't!" but stick to it. If more parents did (including parents of celebrity teens), the issue might not be as widespread as it is in now.

Your Own Drinking Rules

And what if you drink (and chances are you do)? Set an example, and drink responsibly. At least try to stay within the law. Never drink and drive. Always choose a designated driver, and let your daughter know that you do. Do not take part in illegal public drinking, and do not drink to excess. If you do so from time to time, let her know that you understand you erred and that you are paying the price with a horrible hangover. Stress that even as an adult of legal drinking age, you have limits and responsibilities.

The Advent of "Girl Drinks"

Hard Lemonade and so-called "twisted teas" have elevated the chances for girls to introduce drinking into their lives. Liquor sales forces have women in their line of fire, and girls end up there as well with what industry insiders call the "alcoh-pop" line of drinks. The days of having to gag down your father's vermouth for your first buzz are long gone. "Girlie drinks" go down smooth, yet are just as potent as any other beer, wine, or alcoholic beverage. Be sure to stress this to your daughter. Don't let her think that because something tastes fruity, it's okay to drink, even if it has alcohol. In fact, teach her that such drinks can be dangerous because you don't realize you've had too much until—well, until you've had too much.

These drinks can also feel more "socially acceptable" to girls. Make sure your daughter understands that they are not. She needs to see the facts: these drinks contain as much or more alcohol as any other drink and should be looked at the same way. Try to let her in on the secret: the liquor industry is trying to trick her with these drinks. Encourage her not to fall for the trick.

Inhalants

The idea that a quick high could be right under your kitchen sink or in your fridge might be shocking to many parents. Inhalants are used by some girls, and the more you know about them, the safer you can keep your girl.

What Is "Huffing"?

"Sniffing" (also called "wanging") is breathing inhalants through the nose; "huffing" is breathing them through the mouth (as in a paper bag, also called "bagging").

"Huffing" is, put simply, the taking in of common household substances to get a quick, intense, and short-acting high. While most adults are familiar with the use of airplane glue for this use, other items work the same way, including nail polish remover, hairspray, gasoline, aerosol whipped cream, spray paint, and even air conditioning solution. A person takes them and breaths them in, either by putting some in a plastic bag and then breathing that in, by soaking a rag or towel and placing that over the mouths, or by inhaling it directly from the container. The high is like drunkenness; a person slurs his or her words and feels dizzy. Those who huff often repeat it time after time, which can prolong the effect.

"Huffing" has short-term and long-term complications. It can cause immediate, quick inebriation that can lead to other risky situations. Long-term, it's no cliché to say it's killing brain cells. Long-time "huffers" can suffer extensive memory loss and even a decline in basic cognitive functions. Sharing this information with your daughter may help her to think it over when and if someone says, "Try it! It's just from regular stuff. It cannot hurt that much."

 *Question*

Isn't "huffing" more of a "boy thing"?
While some used to think more boys huffed than girls, according to the government's Substance Abuse and Mental Health Services Administration, the number of teen girls who are "huffing" is rising quicker than the number of boys.

Signs of Inhalant Use

Besides noticing things missing in your home (and girls can purchase or steal items for this outside the home quite easily anyway), you will want to look for red eyes, a runny nose, and an odd breath scent as signs. Other signs include weight loss, sudden grade drops, sores around the mouth, and unexplained sickness as a sign. What do you do if you find your daughter has tried inhalants? Immediate and harsh action is warranted. Girls and boys can die from what is called sudden inhalant death syndrome. It can happen their first time or any time, and if your child has done it once, you'll want to get her professional help immediately. It's too dangerous a situation to take as a one-time thing.

Legal and Illegal Drug Use

Remember the mother in the film *Almost Famous* dropping her son of at a rock concert? As he walks in the crowd she spontaneously yells, "Don't do drugs!" around him, hundreds of teens burst out laughing. Parents must find a way to send the same message in a strong and effective but quieter way.

Illegal Drugs

As with every other risky behavior, Hollywood does not provide great role models. The media glamorizes drugs like marijuana, cocaine, Ecstasy, and others. Your job is to cut to the reality that drug use is illegal, at any age. Your first job is getting to know what drugs are out there.

 Alert

Don't base your views on your own childhood experimentation. Even pot is more potent today thanks to special ways illegal suppliers are both growing it and lacing it. Get educated and know what you are talking about.

This topic can be frightening to parents who do not understand what "today's designer drugs" are. Understanding them should not put you at ease, but rather help you have confidence in your vigilance and help you to keep them out of your daughter's life. So what are they? The new wave of club and designer drugs, such as GHB (gamma hydroxybutyrate), Rohypnol,

MDMA/Ecstasy (methylenedioxymethamphetamine), ketamine (ketamine hydrochloride), and LSD (lysergic acid diethylamide), is making the rounds at high school gatherings and college campuses. These drugs are cheaper than cocaine and heroin, and they're relatively easy to obtain, many cooked up right in a kitchen. Most are odorless and tasteless, leaving no telltale evidence for you to detect. They can be addictive, and when mixed with alcohol, they can be deadly. Learn this information and share it with your daughter. However, the "tried and true" drugs still seem to lead. More teenage girls use marijuana than cocaine, heroin, Ecstasy, and all other illicit drugs combined, according to a U.S. government study done in 2004. And you, despite your past, may not even recognize it.

"Legal" Drugs

Every day, on every television station, your daughter is assaulted with advertisements about over-the-counter and prescription drugs that will "make you feel better." The message is simple and dangerous: Take a pill and feel good. Today's teens are turning more and more to over-the-counter and in-the-medicine-cabinet prescription drugs for highs. Cough syrups, both prescription (codeine) and over-the-counter (dextromethorphan) are often a starter drug for girls (there are even Web sites your daughter can log onto with calculators to help her figure out the dose she needs to "get high" based on her body weight!). Be wary of the example you set. Do you reach for a medication every time you have a tiny ache or cough? And be careful of what you keep in your house. There's nothing wrong with a locked drawer for such items, meaning your child would have to ask you for medication at all times.

Steroids and Girls?

You've got it, "'roids" are no longer just a boy's choice. A national study published in the April 2005 issue of *Archives of Pediatric and Adolescent Medicine* found that up to 5 percent of girls now use steroids. They do it for a number of reasons: to improve athletic ability, to enhance their body (via body sculpting), and to become "stronger." Girls can find them on the street. The danger is real. Not only do girls who use steroids tend toward other reckless behavior such as sex, drinking, and smoking, but as most now know, steroids can create rage and suicidal tendencies. Steroids are no longer something parents of girls can check off the list of "not possible."

The "Choking Game"

Why would someone want to force themselves or a friend to faint? For the high. And how would they do it? By cutting of blood supply. This dangerous game is becoming more and more popular with teen girls.

How Choking Works

In many cases, choking is a group game. One or two teens hold the arterial veins on another teen's neck until she passes out, which causes a rush and a quick high. Other times, a teen puts his or her head down and hyperventilates until she passes out, experiencing the same high. To teens, what is happening seems funny and even fun: they barely do anything and get this crazy feeling. And the group dynamic of it can lead to peer pressure. Many parents are just as clueless that this is happening as their children are clueless of its dangers.

How to Talk about It

It all sounds silly and teens tend to think it is harmless, but quite the opposite is true. Choking not only kills brain cells; it can be immediately deadly. A good way to bring this up with your daughter is to ask her to read an article on a teen dying from the "choking game," and then ask her what she thinks about it. You can lead in by admitting, "I have not heard much about this" or "I had no idea this went on. Have you heard of it happening in your social circle or at your school?" Using the magazine or Web article to start the conversation can make it a benign topic of conversation instead of an interrogation directed at her, and may help her to ask questions she'd be afraid to ask if you "knew" she was talking about herself. Such education can go a long way toward helping a girl realize a situation that just seemed fun was in fact, quite risky. In the end, understanding all these issues and their dangers and communicating them without sounding like a worrywart is the challenge. Parents of today's girls simply must be up to it.

When and Where to Get Help

So when do you know it's reached a point your child needs outside help? And where is that help? It's good information for parents to know, even if they never need it.

When It Is Time

Girls experiment. So chances are your daughter has sipped a beer or even puffed on a joint. But it's when it becomes habit that you need true help. Habit would mean, more than once a month, or to such an extreme that she loses the ability to control her situation. Some parents are shocked when their never-drinking daughter is rushed to an ER with alcohol poisoning. This is not a time to say "she just didn't know." That kind of inebriation calls for immediate intervention. Remember, addiction can start young, and if you can help your child stay ahead of it, you may just help her avoid it.

 Fact

There is no such thing as overreacting in this situation. If you insist on getting professional help and you're told that she's fine, you've only erred on the side of caution. To wait too long would be the wrong choice.

You may pick up on your daughter's drug use from rumors, or you may have caught her more than a few times. Whatever the case, once you see a pattern or an overuse, it is time to act. She may tell you that you are crazy: all the other kids drink or smoke way more than she does. Let her know that, as in all cases, you don't care about what any other girl is doing. It is her welfare and future you are charged with, and you will act accordingly. You love her, and you'll do what you have to in order to know she's growing up in a healthy and safe way. If she fights that help, you may need to involve the courts. Minors can be forced into programs and to get help. The courts are actually there to help you. But don't go into it blind. Hire a family attorney who can make sure it ends up being a good thing for you and your daughter, and not a nightmare.

Where to Get Help

While your first call may be to your primary caregiver, he will refer you to a specialist. Dealing with addictions requires a specialist's care. Do ask your primary care team for a referral to a counselor or program that helps girls in your daughter's situation. She'll need someone skilled and caring who knows just how to help girls work past the issues your daughter is facing. It may also be that counseling alone is not enough. Rehab is a familiar concept to teens today, thanks to young Hollywood, but their vision of it may be warped. It's not a place to dash in and out of for a rest; it's a place where a teen works hard to change her life. If you are faced with deciding to put your child in such a place, look for references that matter. If you know of another teen who has been to such a program and done well, reach out to the parent. You'll be surprised how much one who feels your pain is willing to help.

Changing her Life

It might even be vital for you to make some big changes in her life. If her crowd and lifestyle at the school she's at are never going to change, consider a different school. But don't change schools on a whim. Talk to the possible new school about the reasons you want to move her and the issues she has grappled with. It's like the old saying: the grass isn't always greener. You don't want to move her and lead her to think that she can just leave her problems behind. You'll need to back that move with the right program and/or counseling to help her get a clean start.

Chapter 13

Twenty-First Century Issues and Technology

Personal-use technology is advancing faster than you can read these words. Chances are, since this book was written, your child has gained access to an even newer kind of technology, be it games, communications devices, or programs. Because parents are in the dark about some of these things (it seems that teens lead the charge in every new thing), there can be misuse, overuse, and even danger surrounding new technology. Getting yourself not just acquainted but savvy about these things will give you tools to help your child use new technology in a positive and safe way.

Online Social Networks: Keeping Them Safe

The center of the social universe for adolescent girls has shifted. While it was once phone calls, the mall, and a place in town where kids hang out, it is now in cyberspace, which she accesses from her computer. How is a parent supposed to oversee that? By understanding the social network sites and keeping a close eye.

MySpace and Facebook

Unless you live in a cave, you've heard of these sites, currently the hot cyber spot for teens to socialize at. But how do they work? MySpace (*www.myspace.com*) is a public site where anyone, *repeat: anyone,* can set up a "home page" with photos of him- or herself, and details about his or her life. People who are MySpace members (and it's free, by the way) can browse all the other MySpace pages to find people they share hobbies, beliefs, and ideas with. They can reach out and chat with anyone, anywhere in the world. They can post "background music" so that when someone logs onto their site, the music plays like a theme song. Kids today love the kind of networking, and log almost countless hours on it.

 Fact

Although MySpace is a relatively new technology, its reach is massive, with over a million people signed on as members. Its numbers—and its competitors—keep growing.

Facebook (*www.facebook.com*) is newer than MySpace, and has more security features. But parents still need to be careful if their daughter is using it. Facebook started out as a way for college students to get to know one another. In fact, in the beginning, you could only join Facebook if you were a student at a participating school. This meant that, for the most part, it was safer than MySpace. But today, anyone can become a Facebook member. Facebook differs from MySpace in that Web browsers can only see your photo, name, and social group (such as a school or a geographical region your child chooses to say she is part of). In order to see your daughter's entire site or to communicate with her via Facebook, a browser must ask to become a "friend" of your daughter. She will be able to look over her "friend requests" and decide if she is going to let this person into her full page. Like MySpace, Facebook has a spot for sending and leaving messages.

 Essential

Set up your own Facebook and/or MySpace page. Not so you can surf the Internet for new friends, but rather so you have a clear understanding of what the sites are and how they work. Warning: Your daughter will be mortified. But it is for her safety that you learn.

Both MySpace and Facebook offer positive features as well. Some high school student leaders use them to send out messages and reminders about school events. These sites also make keeping in touch with friends from a long distance away simpler and cheaper (no more shockingly high long distance phone bills). Girls getting ready to leave for the first year of college or to a boarding school can get to know classmates a bit before they even get there. MySpace is also a hot place for bands to post home pages to reach out to fans with news on concert dates and album releases and for political candidates to set up informational pages.

Safety in Social Networking

It all sounds safe and good, doesn't it? But here's the rub: because *anyone* can access MySpace, anyone might be reaching out to your child. The more anonymous she looks, the better off you are. So how do you keep her safe? By overseeing her cyber world just as you do her regular world. That often means a battle with a child—she doesn't want you controlling this part of her life either. But you must. Some steps to take include:

- Demand she not use her real name on MySpace. Help her choose a "handle" like "DancerGirl" or something else related to her likes and hobbies.
- Insist that you have her password. That way, you can check over the site anytime you want.
- Read through her "friends" and "wall postings" and make sure you know who each person listed there is. If you don't know someone, ask your daughter for an explanation.
- On MySpace, insist that her page be marked "private." This security measure makes it so that only invited people can view her page, much like Facebook's security.
- Check her profile photo regularly. It is one thing for her to post a photo of herself at the beach with a group of friends. It is quite another for her to post a self-portrait of herself in a bikini. Make sure all her photos are appropriate, and demand that she remove any you feel uncomfortable about.

Instant Messaging, Texting, and Cell Phones

E-mail is now the "snail mail" of online communications. With things like instant messaging (IM'ing) and text messaging, kids today have instant communication at the tips of their fingers every moment of every day. This instant access impacts a girl socially, psychologically, and even academically.

It's an IM World

Instant Messaging (IM'ing) is perhaps the number one way your daughter is communicating with other kids. Most teens log in an incredible amount of hours each day IM'ing one another. IM is available through America Online (*www.aol.com*) and also through other hosts such as Microsoft Windows Messenger. But AOL IM is the leader of the pack. How does it work? Your daughter chooses a screen name and then signs up for the free service. She has a "buddy list" of people she wants to communicate with regularly. AOL gives an option to be private (that is, screen buddies must ask to be linked directly to her) or to be public (that is, anyone can begin chatting with her). Obviously, you'll want to insist on the former. While online, your daughter can chat with as many other buddies as she wants to at the same time. The pace can be furious at times.

Girls (and all kids) are currently obsessed with IM'ing. Think you want to turn a computer off while you are out? Watch for your daughter to have a fit about it, because all kids like to leave their screen names signed on and put up an "away message" so the world knows where they are and what they are doing. They like this, too, because friends can post "away notes" to them, which will stay in her IM box and be ready for her to read when she returns from wherever it is she was going. Such activity can eat up your electric bill. Explain to your daughter why you must shut the computer down when you go out for long hours or travel somewhere.

 Alert

Set time limits for how often she can be on IM and stick to them. Without rules like this, your daughter can easily get sucked into spending hours and hours IM'ing about nothing in particular. IM can eat up a whole day or evening.

Text Messaging

As if all that IM instant access were not enough, kids now have instant communication quite literally in the palm of their hands. Text messaging, done through a cell phone, is the rock star of kid communications today. Because most adolescent girls now have a cell phone with texting services, they can drop short quips to one another all day long. In a way, it's good for you: you can check in on her at any time. But it can be excessive at times, like at family dinner when she stops eating to read a text, or in the car on a family trip when she's engrossed in texting and ignoring you all. Insist on "text-free" times in every day, and stick to them. Demand that the phone be turned off so that you don't keep hearing her phone signal that a text has come in.

In order to text your daughter, a person would need to know her cell phone number. But, that does not mean it's completely safe. Often, a friend will pass her cell phone number on to another person your daughter may not know, and she'll get a text from a stranger. Try to encourage her *not* to accept those text messages, and to erase them and block the stranger from being able to text her.

 Question

Is texting allowed in school?
Most schools strictly prohibit cell phone usage during the school day. If yours does allow it, set your own rule: no texting during school. It's distracting and not good for her learning pattern.

IM and Texting Addiction

It's no joke; the instant gratification girls can get from IM'ing and texting can be addictive. The IM world is like a fake social world. She can say what she wants and not be nervous about it because, online, she need not look people in the eye or see their reaction to something. And the whir of activity when dozens of other kids are IM'ing her at the same time can seem like heaven to a girl who just wants to be "popular."

This is why limiting access is crucial. Think about it: if she's IM'ing a dozen kids while doing her homework, how much can she truly focus on her schoolwork? The constant distraction (and by something she likes much more than homework) can lead to school trouble.

The same goes for texting, particularly during the school day. But watch when you tell your daughter you are limiting her use. She'll be in pain, and this is because these communication tools are truly addictive.

 Alert

> If you see a noticeable slip in your daughter's grades, look carefully at how much time she's spending online at social sites rather than doing research. Chances are, she's not really studying when you think she is.

The addiction comes partially because she feels "Everything is happening online." And truly, a lot is. But she needs to socialize in a face-to-face or at least voice-to-voice way as well. Today's girls recoil at the notion of using a landline phone, but try to get her to every once and a while. The "I am in control" world of cyber social contact should never completely replace face-to-face contact, no matter how much she protests. You can also set boundaries for where and when texting is allowed. No phones at the dinner table might be one rule; no texting while driving in the car with the family might be another. The world seems to have forgotten manners with this new technology, but don't let your daughter forget them.

Privacy and the Internet: Is It Okay to Snoop?

In the cyber world, your daughter can feel like she's out there enjoying life and contact without her parents hovering over her. But the truth is, you can see firsthand what is going on online, and you should. Checking out her cyber world is key to keeping her safe.

Cell Phones

You bought your daughter a cell phone for your own reasons: you'd be able to get in touch with her at any time and she could call you at any moment if she needed you. But somehow, it welded itself to her hand. Take a cell phone away from a girl and she might feel more upset than if you were to force her to march naked down Main Street. Somehow, we've evolved into a society that's always in touch, and your teen is into that even more than you are. There are things you need to watch out for with cell phones. First, most schools do not allow to be turned on during the school day. Make sure she obeys that rule.

 Essential

Teach your daughter cell phone etiquette. Don't answer your phone in the middle of dinner to while taking to others. Do turn it to vibrate when with a group. Don't stare at it endlessly while hoping for a text. Remind her that it's just a phone, and it should come second to other things.

You will need to look carefully at her phone plan and make sure it's set up in the most affordable way for you and your daughter. Some plans charge for texting. You see 10 cents a text and think it's no big deal, but that's for texts going out and coming in. A child can quickly rack up a giant bill. Look for a plan that gives you more for less, and do get unlimited texting. The same goes for minutes. Girls can run up those as well, so an inclusive plan works best. And what about the family land-line phone? When she is home, there is no reason she cannot use that. If you find things get out of hand, and that she's tex-ting and talking endlessly, ignoring all else, you may want to give her a time out from her phone. She needs to see she can he happy without being connected at all times.

"But It's Private!"

Your daughter will argue that her Facebook and MySpace pages are private, like a diary, and that she has the right to a private place. Well, she is correct about the diary, but online social sites are as far from a diary as you can get. Point out to her that when she posted her sites on the World Wide Web, she put them not in a secret corner in her room, but out there for the whole world to see. And that makes it fair game for you to "snoop" at any time. In fact, experts in online social-izing and teens tell parents that "snooping" is a must. Plan on checking her sites once a week. You'll need her password (and if she will not share it, you should ban her from online socializing at all). When you log on each week, check first to make sure she did not use her entire name (a screen name is preferred), and that her address, town or phone number is not posted anywhere. You may want to check also and make sure she does not have her school name there either.

As you look at the people who have posted on her site or visited it, ask her to explain how she knows each of them. Any-one who is not explained simply (for example, "that's Susan's brother") should be removed and blocked immediately. You may learn things via the site that you didn't know. More than a few parents have found out their daughter's relationship with a boy has ended by seeing her "relationship status" changed on Facebook or MySpace. There are photos too. With most kids owning a digital camera, just about every event is captured in photos and then immediately posted on these sites (and never going to be developed on paper for you to see). So what do you do if you see something she was hiding from you (like drinking alcohol or attending a house party you forbade her to attend)? It's fine for you to confront her. After all she posted those photos for the world to see, and you are part of her world. And anyway, what happens on Facebook does not stay on Facebook.

 Fact

As the TV show *How to Catch a Predator* has shown, it's too easy for an unsavory adult to get information on your child via sites Like MySpace and Facebook. Any tantrum your daughter throws about you snooping is worth keeping her safe.

Helicopter Parenting

Technology has given parents a way to know more and more about what their child is doing. By checking out Web pages and reading IM away messages, parents can keep tabs closer than they ever could before. But is this a good thing? To a certain point, yes. Imagine that you read a posting from a friend on your daughter's page that says "see you at the party in the woods Friday night!" Your daughter has told you she's going to a movie. You now can ask her: where is she really going? While she'll call it invasive, you've just kept her from what could be a bad decision. It can go too far though. This "know everything in an instant" world leads parents to think the only way to raise a child is by hovering. Remember, even just a few years ago, we didn't know everything all the time. So if you find yourself obsessing, it might be time to take a breath and let your daughter make some choices on her own, without you hovering over her.

Today's Pressure on Teens: Can You Relieve It?

Sports cuts. The college application process. Community service. Today's teens feel more pressure than any other generation. They are expected to compete and win at a high level. At times, it can all be too much for a girl. Parents need to look at the situation and ask themselves: Is it me, society in general or a combination of both that's built up this pressure?

College Quest

You've heard all the stories. Joey scored perfect on the SATs, captained two sports, and volunteered at the local hospital. But he still got rejected from his top three college choices. It is harder today to get into a college, and parents and schools are sending that message to children at a younger age. Most girls, by freshman year of high school, have begun thinking about what schools they want and what their chances are. While it is true that all your high school grades count when it comes to applying to college, that's a young age to have to think "did this C+ end my chances?" It is important for parents to take a step back and ask themselves, "Is it her dream I'm pushing for her to get or is it mine?" It might just be that your daughter would be just as happy at a small, easier-to-get-into school as she would be at the Ivy League school you've long dreamed of sending her to.

 Alert

Don't push the family alma mater from a young age. While it was once a given that the next generation would get into the school, it no longer is. You don't want her to feel she's let the family down if she does not make it.

It is a good idea to tell your daughter as she begins high school that there are many schools that are lovely and that are not too difficult to get accepted to. Go to some of their Web sites and show her how nice they are and who went there and went on to greatness. Work from the beginning to help her have an initial school that she loves (and is relatively easy for her to get accepted into), then point out that attending that particular school is a given, so any reaches won't be as heartbreaking if she does not make them. And you may want to remove the term "safety school" from your vocabulary. In today's crazy college market, nothing is ever a sure thing. Rather than call something a safety school, just encourage your child to apply to one you know has lower expectations and keep that to yourself. And if you hear her say "it's a safety school," remind her that nothing is a sure thing.

As hard as it is to do, work as a team to block out the propaganda you hear from other parents and teens. Sadly, the bulk of bad information (like, Sue was offered a full ride to College University but turned it down), comes from parents. Today's parents seem to be immersed in their child's future successes, and this can lead to your own child feeling pressure. Be blunt with her and just say it, "Sometimes, people lie." If you can encourage her to block that out and focus on all types of schools, you may take some of the school pressure away.

Social Pressures

Everyone else is allowed to camp out at the beach without parents one night. Everyone else is on birth control. Why, your daughter wants to know, can't she do and be all that everyone else is? Social pressures on teens are huge. From deciding if they want to take part in sex (see Chapter 11 for more on sex and dating), to feeling like they, too, should drink alcohol, girls have many decisions every day and feel peer pressure about them as well. One way to try to help her fight these pressures rather than give into them is to encourage her to join a school group like peer mediators or student council. Remind her, if she plays a sport, that being on that team is a privilege and that illegal or prohibited acts such as drinking alcohol or skipping classes will mean the end of that sport for her, not because you say so, but according to her school's rules.

What if your daughter suddenly wants to dress in a way you do not approve of? The goth look is one example. It's hard for parents to accept seeing their daughter change her outward appearance to something they are not comfortable with. You must show your daughter that instead of being an individual, she is in fact succumbing to peer pressure by adopting the new attire. But in the end, if she's a nice girl who gets good grades and does not act out, you may have to just accept a style you don't like for a while. But do not allow her to get a tattoo. Anything "forever" needs to wait until she is a true adult to decide.

 Essential

Let her have her way with some smaller social pressures. You cannot let her attend a keg party, but you can let her get a belly button piercing, or a third hole in an ear. Showing her you are flexible might help when you have to say "no."

Keeping Up with Trends and Material Goods

When you were a teen, could you even name three brands of designer handbags? Sure, you knew Calvin Klein Jeans and Izod Lacoste shirts, but beyond that, there wasn't much you knew about brands. All that has changed today, and girls know not only a few purse names, but every designer out there. Parents should keep their daughters from believing that their entire identities hinge on brands or things.

She's Got Label Envy

"But Mom, Lisa's mom bought her two Coach bags *and* a Michael Kors dress! It's not fair!" It's tough today to get a girl to see that Gap jeans or any other more affordable brand is acceptable. Somehow, we have become a nation of teens in extremely expensive clothing. Jeans for $150, purses for even more: girls want to have it all. Most families cannot afford this, and end up seeing their daughter suffer from label envy. Label envy can lead a girl to do silly things, like work for months just to save up enough to buy a designer sweat suit she's lusting after. If you can help her to see that price does not make something better, you've accomplished quite a task. So how can a parent do that? Teach your daughter how to bargain hunt and still be fashionable. Try thrift shops and call the wardrobe "vintage." Encourage her to learn to sew and make her own designer label.

 Fact

Parents who see their daughter showing signs of label envy may want to look at themselves. Do you act that way about cars and other items? If so, your daughter could be learning it from you.

Sometimes it is a good exercise to offer to pay your daughter for extra chores in order to earn money for the $150 jeans. Chances are, once she's purchased them and had a chance to reflect on all the hard work she had to do to get them, she might think twice about the value of such a frivolous item and be more comfortable accepting basic labels in her wardrobe. Here's a good idea for back-to-school shopping: instead of going around the mall and purchasing what she picks out, give your daughter a set amount of cash—basically what you can afford for the school shopping—and let her decide on her own. You'll be surprised how much more careful she is with the spending of your money when it feels like it is her own.

Big Box Items

Every girl wants a TV in her room and her own computer that she doesn't have to share with the family. Every girl expects to have her own car when she is sixteen. What if you cannot afford this? Be ready for her to tell you she's the only girl on earth who does not have these things. And be ready to answer that there are many who do not, and that she's going to be just fine without them. You can work out a way for her to use the family car from time to time, and you can mark off an assigned time each day that the computer is hers and hers alone. Same goes for the family television. Try to teach her also that things don't make the person. She may not have her own Land Rover, but she does have her family, her good grades, and her self-worth. And remind her: parents may go into debt to get their children a flashy car; you'd rather save for her college or pay for a family vacation. In the end, it's all about priorities. If she can grasp the concept that some things are more valuable than material things, you've helped her on her way to being a strong, successful adult.

Chapter 14

Coping with Mental Health and Behavior Issues

It has been said that a special place in heaven is reserved for the parent of the teen with mental health and/or behavior problems, but that does you no good here on earth. From ADHD (the American Psychiatric Association no longer uses the term ADD) to emotional issues, parents today seem to have a myriad of possible issues to contend with for their child. The good news is that as many issues as there are, there are ten times as many ways to get help. Recognizing the issue and finding the right resources helps the situation, and most of all, your child.

Loneliness

Isn't everyone lonely and feeling without support sometimes? And aren't the teen years the key years for these feelings? True, but if your child seems to wallow in these, you may be looking at situation that requires more than a new shirt from the mall or an ice cream.

Alert

Be keyed into lunchroom politics. They are at the same time aggressive, hurtful, and often result in loneliness, even in a sea of peers. Talk to your girl regularly about whom she sits with and why. It's a good barometer.

Dissecting Loneliness

Loneliness is not an illness nor is it unique. But when a girl faces extreme loneliness, it can be harmful in many ways. When your girl was little, you most likely made a point of making sure she had playmates. Playgroup, craft time, story time at the local library, and even preschool were ways for you to surround her with different types of interesting children to get to know and hopefully, befriend. Now, you feel at a loss. No longer can you "force" playtime or peer groups on her. As adolescence begins, it is her time to reach out and make relationships happen. So what if she cannot? Different things can get in the way: shyness, a change in friend groups, and even the organization of classes in school can all shift her friend landscape. She can be left feeling alone and lonely.

School-Related Loneliness

School is a virtual sea of possible human contact, and yet, it can be a place where loneliness strikes a girl hard. At school, girls are at an age when a bad hair day or a different choice of attire can ostracize her for a good long time. Of course this is wrong, but telling your daughter that is not enough. If you find she is not feeling part of the program at school (and she does not have to be in the "popular crowd"—a few good friends and a feeling of belonging is enough) that warrants a talk with the school guidance counselor. Often, counselors can help clue you in on what might be going on and what you can do to help (although do expect some frustration; they cannot tell you *everything*).

Even the most "popular" girls can be lonely at school. She might be putting on a front to keep her "friends" and therefore feel no one truly knows her; she might have been one of the "mean girls" only to find herself—to her horror—quickly on the other side of that meanness. Don't assume your daughter will find her way on her own. Talk to her about how everyone feels alone at times and what it takes to reach to others in order to feel a connection to someone. It's a valuable life tool. And remember to drive home that point: a person who has five good, solid friends during his or her lifetime is truly a blessed person. Even adults have times of loneliness.

Loneliness under Your Nose

Loneliness can happen right at home too. Your girl, who once was always the center of the chats at dinner or the laughter at a family movie night, now retreats to her room. She mopes around the house, only coming out to get a cold drink or use a bathroom. The child who once had to be herded up to bed because she loved hanging out with you so much now has to be dragged into even the slightest of conversations.

Make sure your daughter knows you are always there for her. Many parents report that it is during the teen years, even more so than the baby years, that a child truly needs to feel a parent's presence. If you work full-time, schedule a daily after-school phone chat with her each day. Even if it is only for ten minutes, pen it into your schedule and stick to it. And make sure she knows, that if something comes up and she truly needs your physical presence, she *always* comes first in your life. Depend on your parent-radar too. If you suspect she feels alone too much (this can often happen when an older sibling leaves for college, making the after-school hours feel all the more hollow), find a way to fill her time, with sports, a regular visit to a good friend's house, or a shift in your work hours.

 Essential

Set a standard for required family time, be it certain dinner nights or another weekly event and hold the entire family—including you—to it. It is a must-attend and must-participate (as in open up and talk) event weekly.

Online Is No Substitute

She says she's lonely, she barely talks to the family, and yet you hear her tapping on the keyboard constantly. Don't let an online social life fool you or her: this is *no* replacement for good old-fashioned face-to-face conversations and friendships, despite what the twenty-first century teen may think. If you find your daughter is retreating more and more into an online social world, limit her time there and force her to deal with people face-to-face. Limiting chatting and talking to typing and not face-to-face communication starves a child of human contact, something everyone needs to grow and thrive. Force her to be part of the real world, not just the cyber world. And here's a warning: lonely teen girls are the perfect prey for online predators. Be vigilant about whom she talks to and how often (for more of this see Chapter 13).

Anxiety

So if something as simple as doing your hair "wrong" or choosing a unique outfit can cause drama (and even trauma) in the lunchroom and elsewhere, how is a teen girl supposed to avoid anxiety? The answer is simple: she cannot. Everyone feels anxious from time to time. It's human nature. However, you should watch closely how she copes with and processes anxiety.

What It's About

Anxiety can be over many things: grades (or lack of good grades), popularity, boys, making (or not making) a team, how she looks, and how she is perceived. Learning how to channel all this in the right way is part of growing up. If only all girls could know how therapeutic a good, open talk with a parent (or another older more knowing adult) can be, you'd both be a step ahead. And yet, girls like to push back. In some cases, it is girls who do not want to let their parents down and "show weakness" who might stress the most. Bottled up worries do indeed spill over.

In the case of these types of issues, it's fine to share your own daily anxieties with your daughter. It might be refreshing for her to know you stress over the possibility of not making a deadline or the idea of not being invited to a certain social event. But let her know, too, how you work around it. Good planning for things that can be controlled, and knowing how to prioritize what really matters for things that cannot be controlled (like certain social situations) can be ways you can set good and visible examples.

 Alert

Don't ever tell your daughter her anxieties are ridiculous or unwarranted. To her, they are real, and you'll need to help her understand the situation and how it affects her personally (and not how it would or would not affect you) in order to help her.

When It's a Serious Matter

But what if your child experiences anxiety over things she cannot control (like weather) or in a way that is uncontrollable? You may be facing an anxiety disorder situation. Anxiety disorders are more common than most know (and for those who do experience it or have a child experience it, it's like pregnancy—you never notice how many pregnant women there are around you until you are one yourself). Anxiety disorders include general anxiety disorder (GAD), obsessive compulsive disorder (OCD), phobias, post traumatic stress disorder, and panic disorder. GAD presents itself as excessive worry, anxiety, and apprehension on most days for a period of six months or more.

OCD is characterized by constant intrusive thoughts and intense, repetitive behaviors related to the thoughts, both of which take up much of the teen's time. The most common of these obsessions involves dirtiness, while common compulsions include frequent hand washing, using tissues or gloved hands to touch things, constant checking, and counting behaviors. Phobias can be specific—spiders, snakes, heights, tight spaces—or social. Social phobia is the persistent and substantial fear of one or more social situations in which one is exposed to unfamiliar people or scrutiny by others. Social phobia can cause significant anxiety, even panic. Signs of a panic attack include shortness of breath, shaking, fear of losing control, and feeling faint. Often, puberty (and the surge in hormones) can be a time when this truly chemical imbalance presents itself.

 Essential

Anxiety disorders require immediate medical attention. Your health care provider should be your first stop, but expect to have a psychologist or psychiatrist involved as well.

Not all girls who suffer from anxiety disorders require medications, but some do. Work with your medical team and your child to find what works best for her. Don't turn to a prescription as an easy out (many counselors teach things like breathing exercises and visualizations as a way to cope) but if they are needed in the end, think of them the same as a cast. Would you deny your daughter what she needed to heal a broken leg?

ADHD in Girls

Attention-deficit hyperactivity disorder (ADHD) was once a disorder usually assigned to boys, and thought to be highlighted by aggression and hyperactivity. But in recent years, doctors have begun realizing that girls, too can suffer from ADHD, with their own unique set of symptoms.

How It "Looks" in Girls

In girls, ADHD often (but not always) manifests itself with signs of—believe it or not—inattentiveness and withdrawal. Because for whatever reason girls are able to keep things together academically better than boys, they are often able to just retreat and fight the forces of ADHD on a daily basis in a quiet way. Usually, when school becomes more stressful and challenging, girls with ADHD seem to lose control, which is why girls are generally diagnosed later than boys. So what does it look like in girls? Some girls, of course, show the same characteristics as the "classic" ADHD boy: hyperactivity, aggressiveness, and risk taking. Girls with ADHD who show these signs may throw things or jump from high places; they may tend to get in more fistfights than many boys do. Other girls, and doctors claim this is the majority of girls with ADHD, tend to be moody, bored, and unable to cooperate in simple situations. These girls are retreating into themselves as a way to fight the feelings they have.

Another type of ADHD girl tends to be a big talker. This is the type who, some say, never shuts up. And while this sounds sociable on the surface, such girls can be "annoying" to other children because they jump from topic to topic and always want to talk the most. The chatty girl with ADHD may be the most overlooked before diagnosis, because of the cliché of chatty girls in our society. Think Gidget, or even Jan Brady. Girls are supposed to be chatty and funny and sometimes, a bit too much. But if you find your daughter's chatting is scattered, endless, and tends to annoy others, a closer look is warranted.

 Question

If my daughter is moody, does she have ADHD?
Not necessarily. As most parents can tell you, every adolescent girl is moody (and they are lying if they claim otherwise of their child). Look for extreme or deep moods and changes and as always, seek medical advice.

What to Do about ADHD

It's a question that comes up all the time now: are people overmedicating children? With more and more children diagnosed with ADHD, it's hard to know what is right and what is good. For your daughter, you'll want to make sure she is in the care of a qualified medical team who uses behavior management techniques, medication, or a combination of the two to help her adapt to life with ADHD. Behavior management can be as simple as reward systems and as complicated as setting up a schedule for your child. Have a medical team help you to put together a program that works for her and works for you. If the program is supplemented with medications, talk to her medical provider about the chances of working toward a lifestyle and way of working within ADHD without them. If it comes down to the medication making her life better though, you'll want to choose the better life for your child. Another important issue with girls who have ADHD is self-esteem. Girls internalize more than boys. Make sure she understands the ramifications of her condition, and that you'll do all you can to give her all the tools she needs to be successful in life.

Depression and Suicide

Is it possible to be an adolescent girl and *not* be depressed at some point in time? Probably not. But true depression, the clinical kind, requires parental vigilance and medical intervention. Lack of those things in a case of true depression can be catastrophic.

Signs of Depression in Girls

It's a hard thing to separate. True, the chances of depression increase as girls go through puberty, but could it just be a mood swing? Signs of depression are much more prolonged and visible than any short mood swing you may see. Signs include loss of appetite (or large increase in appetite), loss of sleep (or oversleeping), irritability, and an inability to be rational about a situation. Just about every parent of a teen girl can take pause here because almost every girl has her moments. But if you see it over a prolonged time, it's time to take action.

More drastic symptoms can include a marked decrease in success at school (and with grades), a remarkable change in a social situation (she used to go out all the time; now she just sits and listens to "emo" music), or even thoughts or mention of suicide. All or any of these require immediate action.

What to Do

It's hard to not just think, "I was miserable in high school (or middle school) too." But it's better to treat your daughter as a unique individual. As unhappy as you may feel your time was then, your daughter deserves happiness now. And today's society is more in tune with good psychological health that most were in the past. That said, you won't want to ship her off at the first signs of the blues. Instead, try to talk to her about what is at the center of her depressive actions. Find out: Did something change in her social life? Is she upset about your divorce? Has her body image changed in a way that worries her (more on body image coming later in this chapter). You may find it is near impossible to get your daughter to open up to you. This is not because she does not love you; it is because she does. Drive home the point that you are there to help her address *any* of her fears, worries, and disappointments. That is what makes your relationship rich.

If she is unable to put her finger on it or to rationalize and move on from it with your help, it's time to find counseling. Ironically, this is not easy to do. Counselors specializing in teen girls are flooded with requests for appointments, and you may find it takes some time to get a good one. When you do, make sure your daughter (within reason) is comfortable with the choice. Chances are that at first she'll balk at almost anyone. But if after four appointments she's still balking, ask her for input on what type of person she is looking for and renew your search. Better that she open up to someone than continue being closed mouthed to someone she is not at ease with.

 ## *Essential*

Don't fall prey to the "parent should fix all" syndrome. Your daughter is complex and growing up in a world you did not grow up in. If she does suffer from depression, it's not your fault. Just help her get the help she needs.

Suicidal Thoughts

She's at the end of her rope and she screams, "I'd rather be dead at this point!" How is a parent to know when it really means something? Put simply, while you don't need to call 911, no threat to her own body should ever not be taken seriously. The first time your daughter says such a thing, be sure to drive home the power of those words. Tell her to explain to you exactly what she means. If she backs down and says she did not mean it, let her know that from there on, if she uses those words, you'll have to take them seriously and keep her from harming herself. Here's a staggering statistic: girls with suicidal thoughts who have few friends are three times more likely to act on them than boys are. This makes sense. Girls, for the most part, are more socially oriented and internalize things more. In other words, if you've noticed your daughter has a smaller and smaller social circle and becomes more and more withdrawn, you are not out of line to step in and take action, using medical and specialized help.

If you know your daughter is considering suicide or has considered it, you need to make sure she is not in a situation where she can undertake the act. True, this is a time in your life when you thought she'd want more freedom, but in the end, she needs less. She needs support and yes, a watchdog (you) until she's received the mental health help she needs to get through this time. Some warning signs of suicide include but are not limited to the following:

- She says she wants to kill herself or says things like, "You'll never have to worry about me again."
- She has a suicide plan.
- She shows signs of sudden alienation from the family.
- She exhibits a sudden loss of interest in a faith or religion she once cherished or at least accepted.
- She hears voices or sees visions telling her to kill herself.
- She gives away her possessions.
- She is preoccupied with music, movies, art, or writing centered around death.

Bipolar Disorder

While it requires a book of its own, bipolar disorder—and the increase of diagnosis of it in girls—requires mention here. While bipolar disorder is still diagnosed most often in adults, experts are getting better and better at diagnosing it earlier; even in the teen years. Signs of bipolar disorder include excessive mood swings (from giddy to despondent), swings from being overly talkative to being unresponsive, feelings of "superpowers" and then of helplessness. If you suspect any of these signs in your daughter, your medical team needs to know. References to books on the issue can be found in Appendix A of this book.

Eating Disorders and Body Images

It is perhaps *the* issue facing teen girls today. Everyone wants to be thin; everyone judges others on their clothing size. Despite more and more education about eating disorders and their dangers, today's girls (and parents) still struggle.

Anorexia and Bulimia

By now most people know what it is: a person completely starves herself of all nutrients and wastes away. What parents might not understand is what goes into the mind of a girl who chooses to do this. The key is that it may, in the way alcoholism works, not even be a complete "choice." Someone with anorexia has the combination of a fear of gaining weight and a completely distorted body image. She may withhold food completely, or set strange rules for food, such as "Eleven grapes a day and two crackers, chewed slowly." Often, anorexia comes along with other psychological issues, and is centered around control. Sometimes, a girl with an eating disorder may have heard negative talk around her home. It is important that parents teach girls that it is the whole person who is important, not just his or her looks. A girl who weighs a bit more is no less a kind or smart or lovable person than is a girl who is at goal weight or underweight. Don't let her think she can starve herself into love or happiness.

Fact

Many girls who suffer from eating disorders suffer from other mental medical issues, such as depression, as well. If your daughter suffers from depression, be on the lookout for signs of eating issues.

Bulimia, the act of consuming large amounts of food in a short period of time and then "purging" them, either with self-induced vomiting, diuretics, or a combination, is just as dangerous. It is important, too, to show your daughter in no uncertain terms that anorexia and bulimia are life threatening. If you can, have her talk firsthand with a woman who has suffered from it for years. Many die young; many can never have children. All would tell her if they could begin again they'd never sink into their nearly unbreakable habits.

Body Image

How is anyone supposed to live up to it? As the line in the film *The Devil Wears Prada* goes: "Two is the new four. Zero is the new two. Six? That's the new fourteen." Remember when a size ten to twelve was a thin, sexy, desirable woman? Your girl faces a much harsher standard than that. Part of the issue is fashion. While the fashion world is trying to make amends and use "larger models" (as in size sixes!), your girl's role models are all but invisible they are so thin. And as a girl goes through the changes her body sees in puberty, that can be upsetting to the point of depression. What's a parent to do?

First, make sure you let your daughter see that clothes that fit look good, no matter what size is written on the tag. Show her how the size that truly fits her makes her look the best. The number is not the issue; how she looks and feels is the important thing. Second, let her know that if she truly wants to stay "fit," you embrace that. Get her a gym membership but do not let her loose: have her work with a personal trainer who you know embraces a healthy and normal philosophy for the growing teen girl body.

 Alert

There is such a thing as addiction to exercise too. If your daughter eats well but exercises to the extreme, you are facing a problem as well.

If she wants to eat healthy, engage the entire family in the effort. Make sure she eats a good amount of carbohydrates and calories for a growing girl, but help her to learn to eat right (along with you). Show her what a true "good body" is: one that is appropriate to her height and that is comfortable shopping the middle of the rack. Through all this remember, she's listening to you. Too many women—and men—stress out loud about their own seemingly imperfect body image. Watch what you say and how you personally feel. As always, your example will not only lead your daughter, but it may just be the quiet support she needs to embrace her own body.

Chapter 15

Taking Care of You During Her Adolescence

As all-consuming as it was to bring an infant through her first year, you were probably able to think of yourself from time to time. But during your daughter's teen years, that might not be as simple. An adolescent girl's needs can swallow you whole. It is important to remember that for all she needs, you need to take care of yourself in order to take care of her.

How Adolescence Affects You

She's needy. She's emotional. She ignores you and then chides you for not paying enough attention to her. In all that it's easy to want to scream, "What about *me*?" Rather than screaming, parents of teen girls should work at understanding how this all plays on them personally.

Emotional Aspects for You

It's not easy being the mother, father, or other caretaker of a teen girl. First, there's the sense of abandonment some parents feel. For years, you were the apple of your little girl's eye. The sun rose and set on you and nothing was more appealing to her than a long walk or a nice breakfast out with you. Now, she cringes at the notion of spending time with you and often sulks off to her room to ignore you. That's not easy to take. The key here is twofold: Don't be hurt, and don't let it entirely happen.

 Essential

Even if she protests, regular weekly time together is a must. Put something on the schedule weekly for her and each parent to spend together. A quick dinner, a walk around the block—whatever works. And then stick to it come heck or high water.

The hurt is hard to deflect: some girls can think of some cutting, mean remarks to make to parents at times when the parents seem to be most vulnerable. Take this, if you can, as a compliment. She is most likely lashing out at you as a way to get out her angst about a completely different issue. It might be the kids at school; it might be her inability to find a part time job. Whatever, you remain the place she is most safe to act in anger and be forgiven. That said, forgiveness is key. You cannot allow a girl to assume it is ever okay to be cruel and unkind and not at least be remorseful. Sometimes, those "I'm sorry" moments, if truly meant, can be as special as those years when she just plain loved you without these complications. It may also be hard for parents to accept that their daughter has other friends to turn to in times of need now. Being needed is such a vital part of being a parent. Just remember, she really does still need you, even if it does not seem to be all the time.

Physical Aspects for You

The physical changes she goes through impact mothers and fathers immensely, as discussed in Chapters 2 and 3. But what about the changes *you* go through and the physical impact of her teen years on you? When she was a baby, you were younger and late nights (and sleepless nights) for whatever reason were easier to bounce back from. Now, you're older, yet the late and sleepless nights can begin again. Whether you are waiting up for a girl who's been out on the town or tossing and turning over one teen issue or another, these can be sleepless years. It's important to find a way for you to get good rest. If worry and angst over your girl keeps you up enough that it's negatively impacting your entire life (work, social and the rest), you may want to have a talk with your own medical provider about it. They may suggest counseling or medication, or they may just give you ideas on how to sleep better.

If you are a stress eater or a stress starver, you may find these years are rough as well. When you add to that the irony that you need to be showing your daughter healthy food habits these years, it can have an emotional toll on you. Consider, if you are struggling in any way, joining a health eating group such as Weight Watchers or seeing a nutritionist yourself.

It could be your own body changes and hormones mean you need to tweak your eating style at this time in life anyway. And by taking positive action, you'll show your daughter the right way to deal with such issues and at the same time, take good, positive care of yourself. You'll also show her how to deal with body changes when, way down the road, she's an older woman and mother too.

 Fact

Exercise is always a good way to relieve stress and help with sleep issues. Sign up, these teen years, for something new like Pilates or yoga and see if it does not give you an outlet you need and help you feel and sleep better.

Dealing with Worry

What *isn't* there to worry about in these years? She's exposed to situations and events that are new to her (and to you as a parent). You have to worry about her college chances. You want to make sure you are raising her right. But controlling worry is essential.

Worry That's Unfounded

It's not wrong to worry about some things like her first serious relationship or her grades sliding in school. But it is essential to make sure you explore if the worry is real. Let's say you're hearing around town that a lot of kids are lying about going to the movies and going to a drinking spot instead. You worry about your daughter. Is she in the safe place you have been told she'd be in? This is a reasonable worry for a night, but if she's an honest girl who has proven her trust, it's not good to latch onto mere hypothetical possibilities. Your excessive worry might lead her to believe that you don't trust her, which can hurt your relationship with her.

 Alert

Always remember, it's okay to *just ask*. Never be afraid to broach a subject with your daughter, but be sure to do it in an innocuous and non-accusatory way. Her answer may just take your worry away.

It's not good, either, to worry too much about her future. Easier said than done, but the reality is, if you've given her a good foundation and supported her, she's going to find her way, even if it is not the way you expected (like, say, as a pre-med student at Harvard). Sometimes the best thing parents can do is let go of their own rigid view of how their child's future must go and instead learn to enjoy seeing how she chooses her path in life. With all the crazy pressure around colleges today, this is not easy to do. But the parents who can just may find they learn something about themselves in the process.

Worry That's Real

Then again, it is not a good idea to live these years with your head in the sand. As you've read throughout this book and no doubt seen in life around you, there are more dangers and issues for our girls than ever before. Going into denial in these years might feel good for a while, but it's not the right choice. Instead, stay up-to-date not just on teen issues in general (as you are doing by reading this book) but in your own community as well.

 ## Essential

Start or join a "parents of teen girls" support group. It does not have to be formal; just coffee or dinner once a month or so to swap notes and compare issues. You did it when your daughter was a baby. Do it again now.

It's okay, too, to share your "real" worries with her. You don't want her to leave a drink unattended at a party. You don't want her to get in a car with a drunk or even partially inebriated driver. You don't want her to have unprotected sex. While you cannot drill these worries into her, you can find ways to quietly yet clearly let your real worries be known. She might help you relax about them with her own set of standards. At the very least, you'll know that somewhere, deep down, you were heard by her. Sometimes that is all a real worry needs to ease off, if not go away, from your foremost thoughts.

Guilt

It's all your fault. You know because your daughter has told you so, more than a few times. Deflecting and fighting guilt is key to your own mental (and even physical) health at this time.

She's a Master

Where did it come from, this ability to make you feel so guilty? Chalk it up to one smart girl toying emotion and even sometimes emotional blackmail in an attempt to get her way. Guilt can be tossed at you for silly reasons—for example, that she's the *only* girl in your town not getting her own car when she turns sixteen—or for more vital reasons—such as that perhaps it is your fault you and your spouse divorced, leaving her the child of a broken home. Either way, it's important to *not* let her learn to manipulate you too much. She needs to learn healthy ways to get things to work her way and, better yet, how to cope when things don't work her way. You're ability to fend off her manipulations will be key to this growth.

 Question

Can I spoil my daughter by giving in to my guilt about things?

You absolutely can, and this is not a good thing. Girls need to learn that emotional manipulation is never the means to a good end. While it is tempting to just spoil her, do the better thing and help her learn to work through disappointments.

A first step is to not react immediately to her guilt afflicting attempts. Instead, take some time away from the situation, even a few moments, and let yourself think rationally. Take a breath before responding. If you are still not ready to respond, take a walk or drive to give yourself alone time to assess things and come up with a plan and calm reaction. It may enrage her at the moment, but in time she'll learn the pattern, and it will save you angst and harsh times down the road.

When You Truly Feel Guilty

Your work keeps you away from home too much. Your relationship with another person ended your marriage. Or you cannot afford to send her to the private school she wants or buy her the $250 jeans she desires. Whatever the situation, if you cannot shake your guilt, you will need to talk it out with her, perhaps with some professional help. Be sure to think carefully about the situation, whatever it is. Are you truly guilty of an act that requires apology? If yes, do so in an appropriate way. In other words, a ruined marriage cannot be fixed by buying her a car or giving her more freedoms than she is ready for (don't try to be the "cool parent" to make up for things that have no direct correlation on each other). Show her how words and actions can truly send a person on the road to healing and forgiveness. Sometimes, seeing you as an adult forgive someone else of a past bad act can be a powerful experience for a child. It helps her not only to learn to forgive you, but also to learn how to work toward forgiving others and the powerful impact of forgiveness.

Anger, Disappointment, and Acceptance

She's going to let you down sometimes. Be it with grades, actions or emotions, there will be times when you think:

Where have I gone wrong? Channeling that in a way that does not harm her but teaches her and yet does not eat away at you is like winning a triathlon. But with the right training, you *can* do it.

Venting Your Anger

Everyone knows it's not good to yell at your children, and it is never acceptable to strike them. But there are times you are all challenged and yes, there are times when some folks spill over. If you yell in an aggressive way at your child, it's crucial that you make amends as quickly as possible. This can be tricky for you and for her. Your first concern should be her: no parent should raise a girl to think that verbal or physical abuse is ever acceptable. So when you apologize, you need to do it with a plan. It is a good idea to say something along the lines of "I am sorry. From now on when I am angry I will take a walk before we talk it out." It is not okay to say "I'm sorry and I don't want to talk about it again. We all freak out from time to time." Think about the message you are sending: Would you want her to allow a future significant other to act in such a way on a regular basis?

 Essential

If you hit your child, you need help. Seek it immediately and let your child know you are doing so. She needs to see you understand that it is wrong and that there are consequences to your actions. Anger management can be your consequence.

Yet for your own good, you cannot just swallow your anger. Such action causes stress, anxiety, and depression, not good states to be in when you are trying to raise a teenager. Find a way to get your anger out through exercise or the like, and then work at using good conversation and words to reduce the number of angry interactions you have with your daughter. And always assess what it is you are mad about. Is it *really* that important? Sometimes, time heals things and they never really need to be discussed. In other cases, time shows you why you were right to be upset and how you can work it out reasonably. While it seems like you are doing all this for her, you're doing it for yourself too. Wrongly channeled anger hurts everyone, including you.

Managing Disappointment

Even from before she is born, you start building your own set of expectations for her. You want to raise a tennis star or a valedictorian or an artist. In time you have to realize that because you've raised an independent and unique person, her dreams may not be the same as yours, and her skill set may not match what you wanted her to do. This needs to start from an early age, but if you suspect you may be guilty of living your life again vicariously through her, you'll need to take steps to change that immediately.

Such disappointments can be harmful to you and your child. Think of it this way: if you always dreamed of a dancer and she's a tomboy, try to see that as a chance to learn all about softball or football or whatever sport it is she's in love with. And let her know from the start that you love her for who she is becoming, not for the person you expected her to become. Parents who can adapt to their daughter's life as she grows into it can find it to be a wonderful, educational road for them that they never could have imagined before.

Such acceptance helps you relax and enjoy her life as it comes along and helps her see clearly that you love her for the unique person she is and is becoming.

 Fact

It's her life, not yours. As much as you may want her to follow your road, learn to celebrate the road she chooses and help guide her along her own path.

Letting Go: Seeing Her as a Woman

It really will happen. Your little girl will one day be a grown woman, and it will happen in the blink of an eye. It's a time you can look forward to, but expect some mourning on your part as well.

Meeting the New Woman

True, you raised her and helped her through every moment of her life, but your daughter will grow to become the woman she chooses to be. There will come a time you'll have to "meet," and more to the point, accept that woman for all she is and for the person she has chosen to be. This can be a challenging concept for a parent. After all, from the day you first held her, you formed your own dreams for her future. She may have gone in a completely different direction than you hoped at that first moment, but that does not mean she's not interesting, vital, and wonderful to know. As your daughter becomes a true woman, you'll want to get to know all that and not only understand it, but accept it and even celebrate it.

 Essential

Remember those "alone times" you used to force her into as a young teen? It's time to begin them again, only now as a mother with another woman, or a father with the woman he raised. Have a regular "alone adult time" with your grown daughter to keep close to her.

As you get to know your daughter as an adult, treat it like any friendship that is blossoming. Think of how many new ideas and even hobbies you've been introduced to by new friends. You daughter in her adult splendor can do the same thing for you. Listen to her ideas; debate her with respect and consider things from her grown-up point of view. While you should see some mirroring of your self, it is more exciting, and more a sign of a well-raised girl, that you recognize her own individual opinions, interests, and beliefs too. Enjoy getting to know them and consider letting her influence your life.

She's Always Your Baby

Particularly for fathers, it's hard to let a little girl grow up. But remember, in the end, she truly is always your child. If your relationship has been a good one, or even if you've weathered a bad one to come out good on the other side, you've formed a tie that binds. And forever, you'll be the person she can count on through thick and thin. You are forever her parent and she is forever your child. You'll always be close and have time together.

 Alert

Remember, you are still the parent. Even as she is an adult, she does not want to hear about your sex life or other such things. Work on your adult relationship, but remain respectful.

Be ready to be there for her when she's wants to cry or scream; be ready to listen to her fears and complaints about life as an adult. You'll always be that for her. The only change is that now it's up to her to make things better and make things work. Even if you have to watch her struggle (in a relationship, a job, or just in life), you know that the best thing for your "baby," now that she is a woman, is for you to let her listen to your advice and let her know she that she can lean on you. She has to make things happen—for better or for worse—on her own from here on in. If she falters, remind her you will always love her, When she soars, sit back and enjoy the view.

Pampering 101

Feel like you need a spa escape? That's probably because you do. Taking care of your own body and soul isn't selfish; it's helpful to your daughter and your relationship.

Simple Ideas

Take a walk each morning before work, even if it means starting at sunrise. Insist on getting your nails done once a week or so. Join a book group that reads the kind of deep, complicated reading you loved in college. Don't fall behind on your reading time. Such "gifts" to yourself can be inexpensive and valuable at the same time. Pampering and rewarding yourself for your hard work as the parent of a teen girl can make all the difference. And don't hold off your "reward" if you have a bad week. Ever watched world-level tennis doubles players in action? They high-five one another even when they double fault. The notion is simple: if you are trying, you're a winner, no matter how you stumble from time to time.

 Essential

Include your daughter in your pampering from time to time. A simple dinner for the two of you, or a visit to a salon or a ball game together for no reason but to feel good can soothe you both.

Hobby time at home is a good pampering tool too. Learn to sew, paint, weld, or work on cars. Immerse yourself in a project like that for one or two hours a week. If you like gardening, give yourself a new garden. Dig out a part of the yard and make it your new project. The fresh air and hard work can be soothing, even in the toughest of dealing with teen times. It's a healthy and productive escape, and a way to leave everything behind for a bit of time each week.

Pampering Your Marriage or Relationship

Raising a teen can be stressful on an entire family, and particularly on a marriage. That's why you need to work with even more dedication in these years at keeping your relationship (whether you are married, dating, or in a committed relationship of some kind), working well. It's easy for a girl to try to play one parent off another (as discussed in Chapters 2 and 3). Don't let it happen. But beyond just backing one another up and respecting one another, go ahead and pamper your relationship.

 Fact

Date night isn't just for parents of toddlers. You need it now more than ever. Make a commitment to a weekly night out, no matter how hectic things have been at home.

Try to plan a weekend away together, leaving your teen in the hands of another capable adult you trust. (Don't leave her alone! Just don't do it!) Send each other notes of support. Bring home flowers, or send one another flowers to the office. Don't let your teen's life swallow your relationship whole. Exist outside of it, because some day, believe it or not, she will grow up! More than once, a couple has spent decades immersed in raising children only to come out the other end wondering "Who are you? And what did I ever see in you?" Raising children is the ultimate bond, so long as you keep sight of your relationship along the way. The couple that works at that while working at raising children comes out that other end closer than ever and jubilant at the concept of just taking care of one another.

Big Time Pampering

Consider, if you can swing it, heading off for a girl's or boy's weekend away with friends or by yourself. Attend a weekend long ladies' or men's golf or tennis camp. There is nothing like a new hobby to make you feel pampered and like you matter beyond your work as a parent. Book a hotel room and just spend a night alone or as a couple. Wake up alone and order room service and the newspaper and linger over every article in every section. Don't allow your mind to wander to what needs to be done at home or what's going on at home. Take a day or two completely off. You'll come back refreshed and hopefully ready to take on more of the challenges you have to face every day in raising a daughter. Or here's another idea: take turns letting your spouse take the kids away and relax in the walls of your own home. When is the last time you had complete quiet and relaxation in your own setting? That in itself can be luxurious. In the end, the parent that takes care of him or herself is going to be the parent who takes the best care of that growing girl. And that's just plain good parenting.

Appendix A

Resources

Books

Trust Me, Mom, Everyone Else Is Going! by Roni Cohen-Sandler (Understanding and surviving the social life of your teenage daughter)

The Nature Assumption: Why Children Turn Out the Way They Do, by Judith Rich Harris

Unwrapped: Real Questions Asked by Real Girls, by Gina Guddat

Girl Wars: 12 Strategies That Will End Female Bullying, by Cheryl Dellasega and Charisse Nixon

No Room for Bullies: From the Classroom to Cyberspace Teaching Respect, Stopping Abuse, and Rewarding Kindness, by Jose Bolton and Stan Graeve

A Parent's Guide to Building Resilience in Children and Teens by Kenneth R. Ginsburg, M.D., M.S. Ed, F.A.A.P., and Martha M. Jablow

Less Stress, More Success: A New Approach to Guiding Your Teen Through College Admissions and Beyond, by Kenneth R. Ginsburg, M.D., M.S. Ed, F.A.A.P., and Marilee Jones

Caring for Your Teenager, by the American Academy of Pediatrics, Donald E. Greydanus, M.D., F.A.A.P., Editor-in-Chief and Philip Bashe

Your Adolescent, by David Pruitt, M.D.

The Inside Story on Teen Girls, by Karen Zager, Ph.D., and Alice Rubenstein, Ed.D.

Good Magazine Choices for Teen Girls

Seventeen

Teen Ink (written by teens)

Next Step: Your Life after High School

Girl's Life

Web sites for Parents

iParenting
www.iparenting.com

American Academy of Pediatrics
www.aap.org

American Academy of Child & Adolescent Psychiatry
http://aacap.org

About.com Raising Adolescents
http://parentingteens.about.com

University of Minnesota Positive Parenting of Teens
*www.extension.umn.edu/distribution/familydevelopment/
DE7309.html*

Family Education: Parenting Teens
*http://life.familyeducation.com/parenting/teen/43735.
html?detoured=1*

KidsHealth
www.kidshealth.org

Parenting Teen Drivers
http://dalewisely.googlepages.com/ourcontract
(Teen driving contract and information on teen driving)

Web sites for Teen Girls

Empowering Young Women
www.scils.rutgers.edu/~kvander/girllist.html
(A cornucopia of wonderful Web sites for girls)

Girl Power
www.girlpower.gov
(Education for young teen girls, by the U.S. Department of
Health and Human Resources)

Teenwire
www.teenwire.com
(Sex and sexuality by Planned Parenthood)

The Ophelia Project

www.opheliaproject.org

(Catalyst for positive relationships)

Do Something

www.dosomething.org

(Dedicated to teen volunteerism and to helping teens start and maintain community service projects)

Additional Survival Tips

Here are some additional tips and sage advice from those who have been there: parents who have seen their adolescent girls grow up happy and healthy.

- Keep your sense of humor. If need be, come up with a standing joke you can toss into even the most stressful of times. An example is the mother and daughter who, when one is complaining to the other and things get dicey, quip: "What do you want, a cookie?" Laughter, even in the most tense of situations, can relax you and help you turn things around.

  "My best advice is, consider this: This child is not you reborn, but an entirely different person with different tastes, opinions and goals."

  —*Joette Cook, mother of Emily*

- Use chores to calm things down. While your daughter may be enraged that you ask her to rake the leaves when she wants to argue about curfews, the action itself can be meditative, and will give her (and you) some time to think things over.

"When raising girls: Stop, Look, and Listen before you say or do anything that relates to your girl's behavior or appearance. Girls are 'Mothers in Training' and they take everything far more seriously than boys. They listen with ears that are attached directly to their hearts. Your most important role is helping them develop to be great women with a high level of self-esteem."
—Lisa Braun, mother of Kristin

- Do not compare one daughter directly to the other. Even though you've been in the same house and done all the same things, one will not exactly mimic the other. Comparisons can hurt feelings and cause friction between girls in a family.

"I wish I had known that as soon as my daughters reached middle school I could have avoided a lot of conflict had I installed locks on the outside of their bedroom doors and put name tags in all their clothes. The concept of 'sharing' clothes was never equitable and the term most often used when someone was wearing an item that didn't belong to them was 'stealing.'"
—Terry Whitehead, mother of two grown daughters

- Enjoy those moments of peace. Be ready to grab them. If she seems chatty and kind, drop everything you can, swoop in, and have a nice time with her. It will help both of you the next time you are both out of sorts.

"Keep an eye out for signs that she is in the mood to talk and then make time to listen even if it's not convenient."
—*Maureen Hill Collins, mother of a fourteen-year-old girl*

- If she is gains a little bit of weight (and she is still in a truly healthy range), and she stresses over no longer being a size two, take her on an insane shopping spree. Show her clothes that fit, feel good, and look good. Then offer to cut the size tags out if she would like. Teach her image cannot be assigned a "proper size."

"Always, always, tell your daughter, whatever her size, how lucky she is to have a beautiful, healthy body, and that it's important to take care of it with good food, fresh air, and exercise. Prepare food together, take walks together, and be positive. Your unconditional love and acceptance will help her define the feelings she has about her body."

—*Jean Driscoll, mother of two grown daughters, Amy and Alana*

- Don't bring yourself down to her level. No screaming, no sobbing, no theatrics. This can be challenging for a parent. Save it for when you are out of her sight and sound.

"For your own sanity, you need to understand that your daughter is not an anti-social, pathological brat, even though that's how she seems to always be around you. Her friends' parents will tell you they find her to be lovely, friendly, helpful, and cheery—and will be equally

stunned when you tell them that's how their daughters act around you."

    —William Ahearn, father of a grown daughter (who is, by the way, lovely, friendly, helpful, and cheery)

- And one more to get you through these years:

"Some day down the road, when your daughter thinks she is having a hard time with her daughters, remind her that the apple does not fall far from the tree."

    —Jane Hanna, mother of a grown daughter, grandmother of that daughter's two girls

Index